CHIPPENHAM ON THIS DAY

Chippenham

on this day

CHRIS DALLIMORE

First published in the United Kingdom in 2024
by The Hobnob Press
8 Lock Warehouse,
Severn Road, Gloucester
GL1 2GA

www.hobnobpress.co.uk

© Chris Dallimore 2024

Chris Dallimore hereby asserts his moral rights to be identified as the author of the Work.

All rights reserved. No part of this publication may be reproduced, stored in a retrieval system, or transmitted in any form or by any means, electronic, mechanical, photocopying, recording or otherwise, without the prior permission of the publisher and copyright holders.

British Library Cataloguing in Publication Data
A catalogue record for this book is available from the British Library

ISBN   978-1-914407-75-8

Typeset in Chaparral Pro 11/14 pt.
Typesetting and origination by John Chandler

Front cover and title page photograph: Downing Street coronation celebrations, 1937 (Paula Champion collection)

FOREWORD

When carrying out my research for *Chippenham Street Names*, I came across many individual events that I felt should be shared. Most of these didn't quite fit into an etymology of street and place names so I decided to place them into a new collection instead.

I have arranged these events in day order rather than in the order they happened, so that the reader can, if they wish, dip in and out of the book, rather than read from cover to cover. There is one event for every day of the year except for 18 January because almost the same event happened on that day but 86 years apart, so I just had to include both!

    I have used a variety of sources for my research. Old newspapers have been scoured using various methods; the internet, microfilm and original cuttings. A Civic Society Bulletin back catalogue kindly given to me by Tony White, with gaps filled by the late Don Little, was another great resource.

    As with my last book, the online community has been an invaluable source of help. Many of the fantastic pictures you will see reside in their private collections.

Chris Dallimore

JANUARY

1st January 1857

On this day, John Britton died aged 86. Born at Kington St Michael on 7 July 1771, he was the eldest of ten children, all brought up in a small room. Britton's father was a baker, maltster, shopkeeper and small farmer. Both parents died when he was young, so he travelled to London and became apprenticed as a 'collar-man' to a wine merchant.

Later, and mostly self-taught, he found his true vocation as a 'distinguished writer on architectural and archaeological subjects', most notable of which was the *Beauties of Wiltshire*. Published in 1801, it is considered his first great work. He described himself as an example of what 'may be affected by zeal and industry with moderate talents and without academic learning'.[1]

This stone set into the wall of the old village hall in Kington St Michael, marks the site of John Britton's cottage.

Britton also helped found the Wiltshire Archaeological and Natural History Society in 1853, when he donated his entire collection towards its work.

His childhood home has long gone but an inscribed stone in the wall of the Old Village Hall now marks the site - 'JOHN BRITTON BORN 1771'.

In London's West Norwood Cemetery, 'a vast unwrought monolith' marks his grave. This is now a Grade II* listed monument.

Also, a stained glass window in Kington St Michael church commemorates him along with the earlier antiquary John Aubrey.[2]

2nd January 1926

One of Chippenham's most serious floods reached its peak on this date. The high street was submerged up to the town hall, leaving

---

1 *London Illustrated News*, 10 January 1857.
2 Daniell, pp. 235-238.

The flood of January 1926 was one of the worst to occur in the history of the town. Postcard - Paula Champion

the George Inn (now WH Smith) in several feet of water. Many shops were affected and in Bath Road, the level reached into the Nestlé factory. The town bridge became impassable and traffic ground to a standstill. Horses and wagons were put to good use ferrying pedestrians across the river. Hundreds of people stood on both sides of the floodwaters, either waiting to cross, or just in awe of the spectacle before them. Older residents couldn't recall a flood as bad for many years.[1]

A flood-mark is recorded as being used to show the level which the water had reached, but it is no longer in place. A small plaque made of brass, about 7x2 inches in size, was discovered by Peter Mortimore in his garden shed back in the early 1990s. The inscription simply read; 'Flood Mark - Jan 2nd 1926'. How it came to be there, or who removed it from its original position is unknown, as is the actual location of where it originally was. Possibly it was the one now missing from the town hall. Another possibility is that it used to be on the changing room wall at the swimming club at Long Close. Peter Mortimore's father Frederick was a member.[2]

---

1   *Western Daily Press*, 4 January 1926.
2   CCSB 64.

3rd January 2009

This day saw the last of Woolworths in Chippenham, which first opened in April 1933. The administrators were called in after the company accrued £385million in debt. Three days into Woolworths centenary year, 27,000 staff were made unemployed.

Determined to go out on a high, staff in the Chippenham store made their own CD to play on the last day. The last song chosen was Monty Python's 'Always Look on the Bright Side of Life.' DVDs, games and CDs were sold off for as little as 50p each in order to clear all stock before closing time. Some people, looking to grab a piece of history, purchased the store closing signs for nearly £30 each.

The last day at Chippenham Woolworths. Photograph - David Gearing.

One couple, who ran their own business in Midsomer Norton and Radstock, bought the fixtures and fittings, which were installed when the store was revamped in 2005. They were also the last customers through the tills that day.

The general feeling in the town was that the high street was dying. Other shops were set to close including men's clothing store Officers Club opposite.

4th January 1839

An unknown assailant, described as a 'blood-thirsty scoundrel', pulled out a gun on Benjamin Pegler as he made his way to Kington Langley from Chippenham. Pegler, a butcher, had been in town for the Friday Market and had made it as far as the hill, then described as *Yoe-stocks*, when the incident occurred. Fortunately for Mr Pegler, the gun misfired. The motive for the attack is unclear, but a possible theory is that he may have had been involved in an argument at the market; a long held rivalry existed between the men of the Langley's and Chippenham.[1]

'Yoe-stocks' was a small hamlet on the road to Malmesbury. This can be found on later Ordnance Survey maps as 'Yewstock', hence the name Yewstock Crescent used in the housing estate off Bristol Road.

5th January 1935

The sad passing of 'Bubbles' the railway station dog was announced. For eight years he had been a loyal friend to the staff and customers at Chippenham railway station and would act as 'night-watchman'. The black and white sheepdog was seven when he was brought from Gloucester to Mr Self's farm at Cocklebury, though didn't settle and ran off back to Gloucester the next day. Later, he was brought back to Chippenham again so decided, when visiting the station in the farm milk cart, to stay there instead.

Bubbles was formally adopted by the station staff and ticket collector Henry Holloway of Parliament Street sorted out an annual license. A lady customer donated a mat for him to sleep on and an elderly lady from Bath used to frequently bring him food.

Bubbles was particularly fond of children and got to know the times of trains which they travelled on, which he would greeting or sending-off with barks.

He also became used to railway staff shift patterns. One time he went to the house of a staff member, concerned as he had not arrived at work as usual. He was intelligent; only using the bridge to cross the tracks and when taken to a former member of staff's funeral at Lacock, he stood next to the grave long after the mourners had left, as if wondering what was happening.

Bubbles was also a keen supporter of Chippenham Town Football

1   *Wiltshire Independent,* 17 January 1839.

Club, accompanying former station clerk Eric Bulson of Yewstock Crescent, at Hardenhuish Park on match days.[1] He was also a member of the Tail-Waggers Club and wore its badge on his collar.[2] Established in 1928, the Tail-Waggers Club was a charitable organisation that supported the Royal Veterinary College and the newly-formed Guide Dogs for the Blind.

6th January 878

Twelfth Night commemorates the Battle of Chippenham, when the Danes led by Guthrum, forced King Alfred the Great to flee with his army to Somerset. This is recorded in John Asser's contemporary account written in 893;

> In the year of our Lord's incarnation 878, being the thirtieth of King Alfred's life, the oft-mentioned army left Exeter, and went to Chippenham, a royal vill, situated in the north of Wiltshire, on the east bank of the river which is called Avon in Welsh, and there wintered. And they drove many of that people by their arms, by poverty, and by fear, to voyage beyond sea, and reduced almost all the inhabitants of that district to subjection.[3]

By Easter of the same year, Alfred was camped at Athelney on the Somerset Levels. It was there that he allegedly, and famously, burnt the cakes.

NB - The actual date for Twelfth Night depends on how the 12 days of Christmas are calculated, with different Christian traditions giving it as either the 5th or 6th January.

7th January 1907

Ivy Lane School opened, as a replacement for St Andrew's National School in St Mary Street.[4] It was built in Barley Close, with work carried out by Mr Norman of Swindon for £4,000. Although many

---

1   *Wiltshire Times,* 29 October 1932.
2   *Wiltshire Times,* 5 January 1935.
3   Cook, A.A., (2020).
4   Endacott, F.J., (1978).

St Andrew's National School entrance for girls can still be seen just off the churchyard.

had hoped to extend or improve the existing school building in St Andrew's churchyard, the consensus was that the new buildings off Ivy Lane were vastly superior to any previous school built in the town.[1]

8th January 1991

It was the Englands Social Centre's 40th-anniversary party. The hall had not long since been re-roofed with a grant from the Chippenham Borough Lands Charity.

The Englands Social Centre carnival entry, 1949. Photograph - Julie Baskerville. Julie's Mum, Mary Vincent (nee Cole), is 4th from left.

1   *Wiltshire Times*, 5 January 1907.

In 1945, the VJ Day celebrations highlighted the need for a social centre for this part of the town and the idea was raised by Mr William Walker of Wood Lane. It was over 2 miles to the nearest suitable facility at Lowden Avenue.

Although land off London Road was given by the town council shortly after the Second World War, the centre wasn't officially opened until 12th December 1951. Alderman William Ewart Stevens, who was the Wiltshire Education Committee Chairman, and Mayor Herbert Arthur Cruse, presided at this event.

At this time, materials were in short supply, so an old RAF hut was used. Public subscriptions collected from the local community enabled its purchase from a local Ministry of Defence site. Much of the work erecting and finishing the building was carried out by volunteers on Saturday afternoons. Whilst waiting for the completion, the Pack Horse on London Road was used as storage thanks to the permission of Ushers Brewery. Under the leadership of Mr Victor Pullen and his wife Mrs Gertrude Pullen of London Road, £900 was raised in four years from 260 subscribing members.

The social centre still stands, hidden between London Road and Wood Lane. Over the years it has been used by youth groups, for birthday parties, hosting first aid courses, accommodation for visiting groups to the Chippenham Folk Festival and by Wiltshire Council as a polling station.[1]

9th January 1987

An extension to the police station at Wood Lane was officially opened by Mayor Michael May, his wife Barbara and Wiltshire Police Commission Chairman John Church. It included a new custody centre, administrative area, holding cells, separate facilities for male and female prisoners and staff, interview rooms, an exercise yard and

Michael May, who was mayor of Chippenham in 1987 (above). Barbara May at the opening of the Police Station extension (overleaf). Photographs - Michael May.

1   *Gazette & Herald,* 28 November 1991.

an intoximeter.[1]

In 1988, Chippenham Police Division began a pilot scheme tape recording police interviews with suspects. The project was a great success and a further 17 interview rooms were constructed across Wiltshire.

10th January 2020

Sadlers Mead car park closed so that a new development could begin. The plan was to build offices and a multi-storey car park, including 12 electric car charging points. Ultimately, the offices were not built as the company due to occupy them changed their plans. The car park, initially due to the coronavirus pandemic, has not yet been fully utilised.

11th January 1938

St Margaret's Convent School opened at Rowden Hill. A total of 18 children from all ages were on the first roll. Classes were held in rooms within the convent itself. This was a private school open to Catholics and non-Catholics alike. Despite being highly popular and having limited space due to an increase in the population of Chippenham, the school closed in 1968. The sisters stayed on to teach at St Mary's Catholic Primary School, which officially opened in 1962 alongside the convent, and is still in use today.

12th January 2007

This day marked the beginning of the end for Hygrade in Westmead Lane. The meat processing company announced a year earlier its plan to close and move production to Norfolk. On this day, the first 49 redundancy notices were handed out and the remaining 500 staff were told to expect theirs in stages over the following three months. Many of the workers had high praise for their managers, who were as supportive as possible, even allowing some to take time off to attend job interviews

1   *Wiltshire Times,* 16 January 1987.

elsewhere.[1]

13th January 1899

It was the grand opening of Chippenham Cottage Hospital, which was built to commemorate Queen Victoria's Diamond Jubilee. A large crowd attended despite poor weather. The Mayor, Alderman John Coles, was present wearing his chain of office. Sir John Dickson Poynder, a benefactor, also attended, as did Lady Poynder who declared the hospital open. She was presented with a silver key which was meant to open the door, if the weather had allowed. The Rev Canon Rich offered a short prayer and Colonel Helme announced that he had received a large donation from the Ancient Order of Foresters to help with running costs.[2]

14th January 1888

Mayor Francis Edwin Dowding, brewer of the Causeway, hosted a 'capital dinner' for 44 'poor, aged men' of the town at the Angel hotel. The combined age of those who had been randomly selected for an invitation was 3040 years! Dignitaries present included a former mayor of Lowden, along with Aldermen Austin, Careless, Keary and Councillor William Henry Brinkworth (coal merchant of the Causeway).
The Mayoress had organised a similar event for the poor elderly women of the town only a few weeks earlier.[3]

15th January 1900

At the Anglo-Swiss Condensed Milk Factory, a young man named James Hibberd slipped into a tank of boiling water. He was completely immersed before he was pulled out by his colleagues, receiving severe scolds across the top half of his body. Dr Henry Mason Jay was quickly on the scene, but could not do much for the pain, so Hibberd was taken to the cottage hospital on London Road.[4]
Sadly, he died the next day, leaving a wife, Mary Jane, and a four-month-old son called Ernest. Born Henry James Hibberd in 1878 at

1   *Gazette & Herald,* 18 January 2007.
2   *Bath Chronicle,* 19 January 1899.
3   *Bristol Mercury,* 21 January 1888.
4   *Bristol Mercury,* 16 January 1900.

The Anglo-Swiss (later Nestlé's) condensed milk factory. Bank House is on the left.

Winterbourne Bassett, he was living at Sandbrook Place at the time of his death.

16th January 1907

A serious railway accident occurred at Thingley Junction near Chippenham at about 7pm.[1] The driver of the 6.30pm passenger train from Westbury to Paddington, failed to stop at the home signal at Thingley Junction and crashed into the 5pm goods train from Swindon to Plymouth, which was passing the junction on the 'down' mainline.

The force of the impact caused the engine of the passenger train to catch fire.[2] The wagons from the goods train piled to a height of 50 feet in two places.[3] Sides of bacon were found amongst the debris, as an iron cased meat van smashed into the van behind it.[4]

The drivers and firemen of both trains sustained bruises and burns, though Robert Butt the driver of the goods train and Thomas Bryan, his fireman, were the most seriously injured.[5] Butt was pinned between the engine and tender, receiving internal injuries. He was taken, along with the driver of the passenger train and the guards from both trains, to the

1   *Bath Chronicle,* 17 January 1907.
2   *Bath Chronicle,* 31 January 1907.
3   *Western Times,* 18 January 1907.
4   *Wiltshire Times,* 19 January 1907.
5   *Bath Chronicle,* 31 January 1907.

cottage hospital. Charles Powell, the driver of the passenger train, and his fireman John Sweeney, both of Trowbridge, also spent the night there.

Joseph Theodore Kopp and Ernest Stratford Warrilow, both of Chippenham, were sat opposite each other and the force of the accident threw them together, Kopp losing some of his teeth. Other passengers caught up in the incident included the Chippenham Hockey Team on its way home after competing in Warminster.[1]

The aftermath of the Thingley Junction Railway Accident, 1907. Chippenham Museum Collection.

An inquiry into the cause of the accident was conducted by Colonel Yorke, an inspector of the Board of Trade, and held in the first-class waiting room at Chippenham Station.[2]

17th January 1885

The newly appointed Postmaster, Henry Barrett, died at his home at Landsend, Marshfield Road, age 51. During his 20 year career, he had worked as Chief Clerk at Chippenham Post Office and was held with the highest regard by his colleagues.[3]

18th January 1921 & 2007

The Palace cinema on Station Hill was severely damaged by gales which caused £2-3000 worth of damage. A 'hurricane' swept over

---

1   *Wiltshire Times,* 19 January 1907.
2   *Bath Chronicle,* 31 January 1907.
3   *Western Mail,* 20 January 1885.

The Post Office and Hutchings Outfitters. Now occupied by two banks. Postcard was sent in 1908.

the town on the Tuesday morning, described as the 'most severe in living memory.' At 9.30 am the roof began to blow off. Around 10.30 about 15 feet of the outer wall blew inwards. The stage and the cinematography equipment were fortunately unscathed. Had the storm struck in the

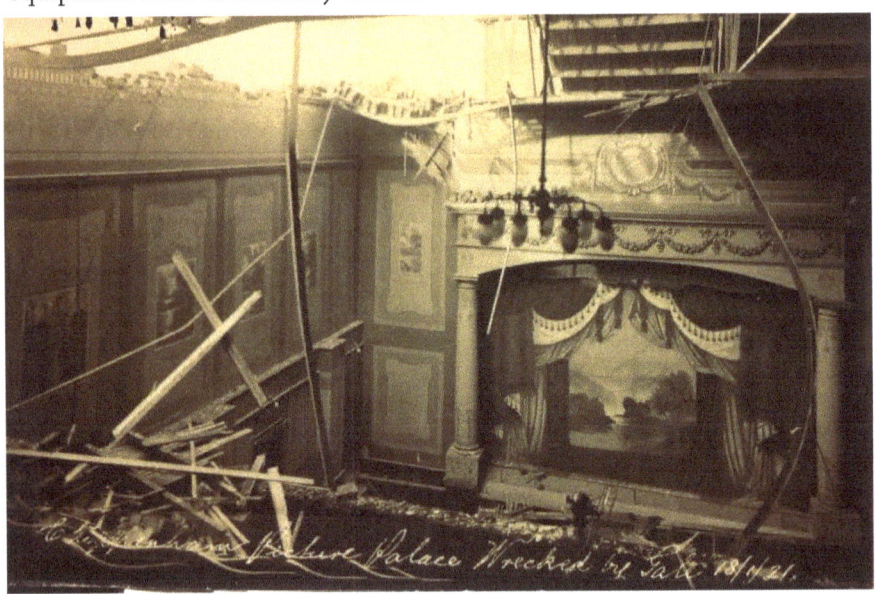

The Picture Palace after it was hit by a gale in 1921. Postcard - Jackie Harding.

evening, when usually there would have been about 600 patrons inside, it would have been a disaster. That evening's performance still went ahead; the Neeld Hall was hastily hired and the tip-up plush seats from the Palace relocated there.

The re-opening of the Palace took place on 28th July of the same year. Mayor Arthur Moyle Stevens performed the opening. Circuit General Manager Mr Van Den Bergh stood in for Mr Albany Ward who was unable to attend due to illness.

Exactly 86 years later in 2007, Chippenham railway station had to be closed after damage to the roof during sustained powerful gales in the afternoon. A top section of the main footbridge blew onto the tracks and the remaining roof had to be quickly made safe and the debris removed from blocking the line. The station was closed and replacement bus services and taxis were used to help connect commuter journeys.[1]

19th January 1918

Another flood makes the town bridge impassable for those wishing to cross on foot. There were many severe floods in the town, especially

The flooded High Street outside the Co-operative building (until recently Wilko). This postcard is from 19th January 1918.

1   *Gazette & Herald*, 18 January 2007.

before the implementation of defences in the 1960s. The postcard from 1918 shows a woman wearing a face mask. These were worn by many in 1918 due to the Spanish Flu, but as it didn't reach the UK until the following spring, we can assume it was due to the smell of overflowing drains![1]

20th January 1972

In Wood Lane, arsonists set fire to Westmead Junior School Headmaster's office. Part of an adjoining classroom was also damaged. The logbooks and admissions register dating back to 1858 were all destroyed.

The fire started around 4.50 am and was spotted by Police Constable Colin Cowley who quickly called the fire brigade. The school had to close for two days and the repair bill came to £7000 with a further £800 needed to replace books.[2]

Two weeks before, a break-in at Hardenhuish School caused hundreds of pounds worth of damage. Mayor Leonard Doggett offered a £25 reward for information that would lead to the culprits being brought to justice and called, perhaps controversially, for vigilante groups to be formed to 'protect County property'.

At Westmead, a tin marked 'Spirit Duplicator for Speed' was found. Entry was gained by hacking away the putty at a window, which was the same method used at Hardenhuish.

There were 170 children who attended the school, 60 of which turned up as usual the next day not knowing the fire had occurred and had no parents at home, so had to be accommodated over the road at Westmead Infants.

21st January 1950

The first annual Chippenham to Calne Road Walk Race took place, with Mr Gerald H Gregory of Trowbridge winning in a time of 46 mins 17 secs.

About 30 years earlier, well known Calne resident Gordon Fred Smith, managed the distance in 1hr 8mins, with no training, as a result of a bet. Inspired by Smith, Trowbridge Athletic Club took up

1   CCSB 64.
2   Endacott, F.J., (1978), pp 12-13.

the challenge of organising a race and for this first event there were 38 entries.[1]

A large crowd watched the competitors set off from Market Place. Chippenham's Mayor Alderman Norman Edward Park set them off whilst the Calne Mayor had the job of referee. The finish line was at Calne Community Centre.[2]

The competition 'ran' until 1999.

22nd January 1874

There was a party to celebrate a royal wedding, which took place the following day. This was between the Grand Duchess Maria Alexandrovna of Russia and Alfred, Duke of Edinburgh, the second son of Queen Victoria.

A ball held in the town hall, was attended by about 130 people from the town and surrounding area. A quadrille band from Bristol provided music. Decorations kept from a previous ball were used but the floor was polished especially. Dancing began at 9pm and continued through the night until between 4 and 5am! Richard Careless, proprietor of the Angel Hotel, supplied the food and drink.[3]

23rd January 1891

Earl Cork presided over a meeting of the Great Western Railway Temperance Union at the Temperance Hall in Foghamshire. It was his opinion that 'no other class of worker should ensure their sobriety more than a railway employee, as they had lives

The Temperance Hall is now a centre for martial arts

1   Callow, H., (1989)
2   *Wiltshire Times,* 28 January 1950.
3   *Western Daily Press,* 24 January 1874.

of millions in their hands over the course of a year.' He argued that although temperance was good, total abstinence was safest and best to guarantee the safety of others. He went on to say that it was important to set the example; to show others the benefits of an alcohol free life. Also present at the meeting were Wesleyan minister Reverend William Woodman Treleaven, Mr Williams the Stationmaster, Mr Clutterbuck of Hardenhuish Manor and Alderman Harris of Calne.[1]

24th January 1936

Several hundred pounds worth of damage was caused by a fire in Foghamshire. Approximately 7-800 gallons of oil fuelled an explosion in a two storey building used as a store by Messrs William Charles King & Son, Ironmongers. The fire brigade, led by Second Officer Harry Slade, managed to pull out a motor car unscathed. A plentiful supply of water was obtained from the brook behind, but the flames were fierce, and eventually the whole building was burnt out. It was believed that the cause was a short circuit in the electrics of a van parked inside. The flames reached a 'tremendous height' and when one of the windows blew out, the glass smashed a window in the telephone exchange 25 yards away.[2]

Advertisement for Messrs. WC King & Son, Ironmongers who kept stores at Foghamshire.

25th January 1990

The Burns' Day storm is often overlooked because of the famous event in 1987, of which BBC weatherman Michael Fish was credited for failing to predict. That storm struck during the night and killed 18 people in the UK.

1   *Bristol Mercury*, 26 January 1891.
2   *Western Daily Press*, 27 January 1936.

Even more tragic though, was the Burns Day Storm of 1990, which made landfall in the daytime and was responsible for the deaths of 47 people. It was estimated that four million trees were felled and £2.5 billion of damage was caused. Wiltshire was one of the worst hit parts of the country.

The one fatality in Wiltshire occurred at a primary school, where an 11 year old girl was killed when the roof of her classroom collapsed. The school, Grange Juniors in Swindon, had to be completely rebuilt.

Maud Heath's head was blown off her monument at Wick Hill, Bremhill. Photograph - Dave Edwards.

Hurricane-force winds caused 21 trees to come down in John Coles Park which needed to be closed for the first time in its history. There were scenes of 'utter devastation' on Rowden Hill as huge trees crashed down close to houses. Telephone and electricity lines were knocked down in some parts of the town.[1]

Sheldon School had to close when part of the administration block roof was ripped off by the wind. Similarly, at Hardenhuish School the roof of the Design and Technology block blew away.

Ten children from Sheldon School had to be taken home in the back of a police van as their bus to the villages had been cancelled. They were given cups of coffee and chocolate by police officers.

The top half of a 40ft fir tree was snapped of in St Andrew's churchyard.

1   *North Wilts Herald,* 31 January 1936.

Hill Corner Road area was probably the worst affected for power outages although Greenway Gardens and parts of Pewsham were without power for five days.

One classroom had its roof ripped off at Frogwell Junior School and was out of action for several weeks afterwards.

A nine year old girl had to be taken to hospital when she was showered with glass during a PE lesson in the hall at St Mary's School. She needed nine stitches in her thigh and four in her foot. The roof of the sports shed had ripped off and hit the side of the hall. Several other children, including the headteacher's daughter suffered minor cuts. Both schools had to close.

Chippenham High Street and Bath Road both had to close because of flying debris, and older houses on New Road lost roof tiles.[1]
The roof of the Spar shop on London Road was stripped of nearly all its tiles and Frank's grocery shop on The Bridge lost its roof.

Wood Lane police station struggled due to the volume of calls with only incoming available and no light or heat for staff. Off duty staff, trainees and even members of the public were all called upon to help out and did so admirably.

26th January 1838

For the third time within a 'very limited period' a fire had broken out at the Sun Inn Public house in the Shambles. This time however, it was burnt to the ground and adjoining buildings were also damaged. The fire started between 1am and 2am, and raged 'with the greatest fury', despite the efforts of firefighters from Chippenham and Corsham. Presumably there was insufficient water pressure to fight the fire, as was often the case.[2]

27th January 1901

During a severe gale a chimney fell at the Temperance Hall leading to a narrow escape for the hall keeper. The wind blew with 'terrific force' from the west, uprooting trees and dislodging slates and tiles from rooftops.

The hall's flagpole, which was flying the Union Flag at half mast due

1   *Wiltshire Times*, 2 February 1990.
2   *Bath Chronicle*, 1 February 1838.

to the death of Queen Victoria on the 22nd, was carried away by the wind.

At about midday, a chimney and a portion of the roof was struck by the wind and crashed through to the large hall on the first floor. The hall keepers apartment was below. The beams and other debris fell into the kitchen where widow Sarah Annie Merryweather, the hall keeper, was making dinner. She was knocked to the floor and pinned down. Miraculously, she was still alive and her son, Albert Edwin Merryweather, was able to pull her out from underneath, just before more timber and brickwork began to fall.[1] The fireplace in the kitchen ignited so the fire brigade were called, with Captain Phipps and his men soon having things under control. Residents in the adjoining properties had to evacuate themselves and their possessions as a precaution.[2]

Sarah Merryweather, Keeper of the Temperance Hall in Foghamshire. Photograph - Desiree Prakash

The Temperance Hall has had many uses over the years since it was built in 1863. During the Second World War it was used as a food office and as Home Guard HQ.

28th January 1925

On this day, Miss Mary Carrick Moore died at the age of 86. She was the great niece of General Sir John Moore, who died in command of the British Army at the Battle of Corunna in Spain in 1809, during the Napoleonic War. In her will she bequeathed £100 to the Cottage Hospital fund.[3]

She had already donated paintings by Thomas Lawrence of her famous uncle, and his brother Admiral Sir Graham Moore, to the National Portrait Gallery in 1898.

1   Some information from 1901 Census.
2   *Wiltshire Times*, 2 February 1901.
3   *Wiltshire Times*, 25 April 1925.

Moore was unmarried, so was the last lineal descendant of her family. The 'Mary Carrick Moore Fund for the Poor' charity was set up with her estate, for the 'benefit of the poor of the parish of Cobham.' This only closed in 2014, when all the funds were finally spent. The family seat was at Brook Farm in Cobham, Surrey.

29th January 1872

Permission was given to the General Post Office to erect a line of poles along the Corporation's stretch of London Road, for the purpose of the direct telegram route from London to Bristol.[1] The application was made by the Postmaster General to continue the route of the telegraph wire from Chippenham to Stapleton Road in Bristol.[2]

30th January 1836

The Local Government Act saw 'Improvement Commissioners' introduced, responsible for lighting, clean streets and policing. Three weeks earlier, the borough council was appointed as the 'Watch Committee'. At a meeting on this day, the first policeman for Chippenham was appointed - Constable John Gibbs. His salary was 12s 6d a week.[3]

In the instructions set out by the Commissioners of the Chippenham Improvement Act of 1832, police officers or street keepers were to be sworn in with the power of constables. They were required to be on duty every day from 6am-9pm, with night watchmen from 8pm-6am. Included in the list of potential offences that they would need to act upon or prevent were; 'the dusting of carpets, the flying of kites and driving of hoops'. To enforce the rules, the constables were equipped with a bludgeon and a rattle.

31st January 2018

It was the final day of trading for the Revelation Christian Resource Centre in River Street. After 33 years the shop finally closed at 4pm.[4] The business was first opened on 4th March 1985, by Sue and Syd Howe

1 Goldney, p.175.
2 *Devizes and Wiltshire Gazette*, 8 February 1872.
3 Chamberlain, J.A., (1976).
4 *Gazette & Herald*, 6 January 2018.

Mural on the side of the former Revelation Christian Resource Centre.

at 29 Causeway, with Jill Dann, former Chippenham Mayoress and member of St Paul's Church officiating. The shop had a bed-sit above for Christians in need of temporary accommodation. It was staffed mainly by volunteers and became a charitable trust in 1990.

Chippenham Civic Society recognised the shop in River Street at their annual conservation awards. A certificate of merit was awarded for the mural which was inspired by an idea of the late Rev Percy Tucker. The 'Millennium Mural' was created by artist Anita Andrews based on designs suggested by children from Langley Fitzurse Primary School. It was painted on a series of plywood panels and is 20ft wide by 10ft high.

FEBRUARY

1st February 1976

The tracks at Chippenham Railway Station were realigned to allow high speed trains to pass through. After this time, the first platform was taken out of service, explaining the unused platform which exists today. It couldn't accommodate the entire length of the new Intercity 125 trains, on which all doors opened at the same time, potentially allowing passengers out onto a large drop! The track had to be

The unused platform at Chippenham Station is too short for modern trains.

straightened and concrete sleepers installed. The footbridges had already been raised in preparation.

2nd February 1742

Chippenham was at the centre of British politics, when a by-election loss was seen as a vote of no confidence in Prime Minister Robert Walpole, who then resigned.

3rd February 1782

At about 2am in the morning, the post boy carrying the mail from Marlborough to Chippenham was a mile and a half outside of town, when he was stopped by a lone highwayman. The boy was robbed of a bag of letters destined for Bath, Warminster and Frome.[1]

Described as 'a person with something over his face, mounted upon a very good horse', he fled at full speed into Chippenham. A £200 reward was offered for the capture of the man. Any accomplice who came

---

1   *Salisbury & Winchester Journal,* 11 February 1782.

forward with a name would also be able to receive the reward along with 'his majesty's gracious pardon'.

William Pease (sometimes recorded as Peare), a native of Cricklade, was discovered to be the perpetrator. Pease was described as a 'fine young fellow, about 23 years of age, 5 feet 10 inches…by trade a blacksmith'. He was committed to Gloucester Castle to await trial for the crime, but was able to escape whilst confined to a room at the very top of the castle. He broke through onto the rooftop and then made his descent using a rope which had been secured by somebody on the outside. Pease was later caught committing a similar crime in Stroud, then later tried and sentenced in Salisbury. Whilst awaiting execution at Fisherton Gaol, he almost escaped again. Having drugged the guards with outside help, he was able to free himself from his shackles. Almost outside, he was discovered and resecured, this time with an additional 'collar of iron' around his neck and chained to the floor.

The execution took place on 19th August 1783. It was reported that he went to the gallows with a 'customary nosegay' of flowers, which his hand still tightly gripped after his body was cut down. Death did not end Pease's punishment. His body was enclosed 'in a suit of chains made with great ingenuity, by Mr Wansborough of Salisbury', taken back to Chippenham and fixed to a gibbet close to where the robbery had taken place. This was a grim warning to others not to commit similar crimes. The following is an excerpt of a poem published after Pease's death, believed to be written by his sweetheart;

> For me he dared the dangerous road,
> my days with goodlier fare to bless,
> he took but from the miser's hoard,
> from them whose station needed less.

4th February 1933

There was a burglary at Ferfoot, the home of Mr William Goold Slade. A maid called Winifred Laverton, came downstairs at 6.20am as she could hear footsteps, but the intruder had already escaped through the drawing room window. Entry had been gained by breaking a small pane of glass in the hall window and lifting the latch. Whilst ransacking all but the dining room, the thief stole cigarettes, matches and an 'electric torch' from the 'smoke-room'. He woke the maid by accidentally knocking over a bowl of potpourri.

John Bernard, 35, of no fixed abode, was later charged with breaking and entering. PC Roberts of Calne Police had heard about the break-in and stopped the accused walking up Tunnel Hill at 8.40am. Bernard claimed to have bought the stolen items off a man he had met on the road that morning. He even had the audacity to smoke one of the Wills Gold Flake cigarettes on his way to the police station. He was later committed for trial at Wilts Quarter Sessions in Salisbury.

Ferfoot was built in 1902 as part of an eight acre estate, with six bedrooms, attractive gardens, paddocks, a stabling block and an orchard. It was sold to a development company for £80,000 in 1972 after Mr Slade died. The house is now part of a care home for the elderly.

5th February 1891

A Great Bustard was shot in Chippenham, which was an extremely rare event as the bird had been wiped out in Great Britain by the 1840s. This was one of a handful of reported visitors spotted across several counties between 20th December 1890 and 7th February 1891.

Mr Wood and his brother, both of 'Langley Green', were searching for wild geese at around 10am at 'Alington Mead on the banks of the Avon, behind Kellaways Mills'. On seeing the Bustard flying towards them they assumed it was a wild goose. It wasn't until they shot the bird, they realised what it was. Mr Wood was quick to send it to 'Foot, the bird-stuffer' at Bath. It measured five feet from wingtip to wingtip and weighed nine pounds. Evidence of its diet in the stomach contents, which were sent to Kew Gardens in London for analysis, showed that the bird must have only been in the UK for a few hours.

'Gertrude' the friendly Great Bustard at Stonehenge, April 2019

In 2011, conservationists reintroduced 50 Bustards on Salisbury Plain from orphaned Russian eggs.

6th February 1966

There was an attempt to derail the 7.30 train from Bristol to Paddington using concrete slabs, about a mile from Chippenham station, from the high embankment approaching Lowden Bridge. The train was scheduled to stop, so luckily was slowing down when it collided with the slabs, that led beside the line before the vandals moved them. Had the train traveled faster, the incident could have been much more serious. On arrival at Chippenham a report was made and a 'light train' was sent back in the direction of Thingley Junction to check the line was clear. It made it back to Thingley without incident, but on its return to Chippenham Station, more concrete slabs were found to have been placed, this time on both the 'up' and 'down' lines, on the stretch between the Bath Road and Lowden bridges. During this time the police were carrying out a search for the culprits. In the end, the next train from Bristol was delayed by 25 minutes, but fortunately no one was hurt.[1]

7th February 1953

An American bomber, one of the worlds largest aircraft at the time, crashed in woods at Nethermore near Lacock. The B-36, allegedly with top-secret military equipment, flew 30 miles over North Wiltshire without a pilot or crew. It fortunately missed Chippenham and crashed in a remote location near Pitters Farm near Sandy Lane. Nobody knew why the crew bailed out so early or what was actually wrong with the aircraft. This mystery is still unexplained.

The plane had taken off as part of a group of 17 flying from Texas to RAF Fairford. Due to poor weather conditions over the Atlantic Ocean the planes were running low on fuel. Pilot Lieutenant-Colonel Herman Gerick missed two ground control approaches so had to circle over Fairford. For some reason he chose to bail out even though some fuel remained. The 15 men jumped out over open country, landing scattered across three different counties; Wiltshire, Oxfordshire and Berkshire. The Fort Worth Star Telegram dated 8th February 1953, reported that a

1   *The Times,* 7 February 1966.

fire had broken out on board before the bail out. No one on the ground was hurt and fireman were quickly on scene to put out burning trees. All 16 other planes landed safely at RAF Fairford.

Malcolm Heath of Lacock was a witness to the event. He heard a strange throbbing noise followed by three loud thumps.

The investigation was not made public but reasons for the crash that have been suggested include crew undermanning and inexperienced personnel at RAF Fairford air traffic control.

Most of the crew involved in this incident, later died in another B36 crash at El Paso, Texas in December 1953.[1]

8th February 1794

Plans were first put forward for the construction of the Chippenham arm of the Wiltshire and Berkshire canal. Work could not start until an Act of Parliament had been passed.[2] The Borough gave permission for the canal to pass through Borough Lands.[3] Two and a half acres at Englands, valued at £229 10s, were taken for the canal and towpath.[4]

9th February 1820

After King George III died on 29th January, King George IV took to the throne. At the next meeting

'Double Bridge' on the approach to Lacock. Beautifully restored by the Wilts & Berks Canal Trust and opened by HRH The Duchess of Cornwall in 2009. Photograph - Ray Alder.

1   Research by historian Paul Moran.
2   Platts, Arnold, (1947), p.82.
3   Alder, p.11.
4   Platts, p.82.

of the Burgesses of the Borough, a proclamation was read announcing the new king. A hogshead of strong beer was given by the burgesses to the constables, the band and clubs who attended.[1]

10th February 1892

At Chippenham Police Court, two homeless men received punishment for a minor crime. George Hall from Staffordshire was charged for being drunk and disorderly in the town. Described as 'a tramp', no sympathy was given as he was sentenced to a month in prison. Pensioner William Wood was remanded after stealing a loaf of bread worth 3d from the Co-operative Society. He described himself as being 'on tramp'.[2] This shows how unacceptable 'vagrancy' was seen at the time, yet little was done to actually help the situation of the homeless, especially for those outside of the parish.

The Co-operative Society store was in the high street (until recently Wilko) in a former private house. Opened in 1890, it included a 'monster oven' capable of baking 600 loaves of bread at one time.

A Co-operative Society trade token which was worth one loaf of bread to the holder

11th February 1942

Patrick McGuire of no fixed abode was commuted for trial at the Wiltshire Quarter Sessions, after a special police court held at Chippenham. During the black-out, Police Sergeant Cox was on duty in the Market Place when at 11.15 he heard the sound of glass break in the high street. He ran to the scene to find McGuire standing at the entrance to River Street. He gave chase but lost him near the market yard entrance. Returning to the scene of the crime, PS Cox discovered that the window of Burtons was smashed and found a display stand in River Street. He then called to the Police Station to request that road blocks be set up. Around 12.15, PC Toogood of Corsham stopped a lorry in which McGuire was a passenger. He was wearing a brand new blue overcoat which matched the one missing from Burtons, tags still attached. McGuire

1   Goldney.
2   *Western Daily Press*, 11 February 1892.

claimed he bought it from a soldier only a couple of hours before. Ernest John Jefferies, manager of Burtons in Chippenham, said the coat was worth £3 15 shillings.[1]

12th February 1957

Thieves broke into the Gaumont Cinema in Timber Street, but only gained access after their third attempt. Once in, they blew open the safe in the manager's office with explosives, and took the contents, reported as not exceeding £100.[2]

13th February 1998

Operation Crusade began, and for the next two days, Chippenham became launched onto the national news scene. An unexploded Second World War bomb was reported by Tony Crew, who as a child in 1942, witnessed a bomb falling on a field near Stanley Lane. His account was dismissed at he time, but he felt compelled to highlight his memory, when plans were made to build a secondary school there.

Upon investigation, contractors discovered two unexploded bombs. Police set up an 800 metre cordon, with 500 homes needing to be evacuated. Over 1100 people were displaced until the job was done, many having to stay at RAF Lyneham. The smaller of the two devices, weighing 500lb, was diffused safely, but the 1000lb device, nicknamed 'Fat Boy', had to be detonated in a controlled explosion. This was successfully carried out at 13:15 on the 15th February.

Fragment of the larger bomb discovered before Abbeyfield School was built, here on temporary display at Chippenham Museum. Photograph - Ray Alder.

1   *Wiltshire Times*, 28 February 1942.
2   *Wiltshire Times*, 15 February 1957.

Emergency financial assistance towards the cost incurred by North Wiltshire District Council was granted under the Bellwin Scheme.

14th February 1537

Cistercian Stanley Abbey and its lands were sold by King Henry VIII to Sir Edward Baynton for £1200 as part of the dissolution of the monasteries.

Traces of the abbey can still be found in a garden just off the disused railway line at Stanley. Here, the monks used the river to form fish ponds and power a mill. The mill was still working, and an abutment from the original bridge was still in existence, as late as the early 19th century. The ownership of the abbey descended to the Starkeys of Spye Park and later the land was passed to the Marquis of Lansdowne of Bowood.[1]

Encaustic tiles and sculptured stones were salvaged from the ruins and assembled in an oratory at Bremhill vicarage garden by William Lisle Bowles.[2] Others were sold to the Parish Priest of St Edmund's Catholic Church in Calne in 1955 by the owner of Stanley Abbey Farm. These are on display in the church porch and the presbytery garden.[3]

15th February 1953

Reginald Wild, of 1 Ashton Road, carried a hundred weight of coal from Chippenham to Calne in a record time of 2hrs 15mins. In doing so he regained the coal-carrying championship title from Cornwall.

A few weeks previously, for a bet, he went as far as the top of Derry Hill totalling 3 and a half miles. Calling for a challenger to beat his distance, Ernie Miners from Truro, carried his sack 4 miles. To regain the record, Reg set himself the target of getting to Calne which is a distance of 6 and a half miles. Despite being small and of slight build, he carried the load from his employers, Messrs Mortimore & Son of the railway station yard, to Calne Town Hall without once putting the sack down. A native of Calne, he was greeted there by a huge crowd including his elderly mother.

Reg admitted to smoking 30 cigarettes a day, but to only having one on the journey! He had no special training other than missing his usual

---

1   Daniell, pp.48-54.
2   Daniell, p.53.
3   saintedmundscalne.org.uk

Invoice from Mortimore's, 1936

Saturday beer the night before.[1]

In September, he managed to carry the hundred weight of coal from Chippenham to Bath, 13 miles in total. Sadly, he died at Chippenham Isolation Hospital later that year, after being ill for some time and unable to work.[2]

16th February 1929

At 7 am, Frederick Cook of Factory Lane, found Reginald Hedges of Melksham lying on his back in the snow, unconscious, with a gun in his possession and a gunshot wound in the left side of his head. This was just outside the entrance to the pedestrian tunnel under the railway line, at the Ivy Lane School end.

His fiancée, Violet Collier of Unity Street had known Reginald for three years and they had become engaged a few months before the incident.
The pair often had 'tiffs' which would sometimes result in threatening behaviour from Reginald. Violet eventually had enough and decided to break off the engagement, when three weeks earlier he threatened to hit her.

Despite returning her ring, Reginald made persistent attempts to contact Violet and threats of violence by letter when he did not receive

1   *Wiltshire Times*, 21 February 1953.
2   *Wiltshire Times*, 26 September 1953.

favourable replies. Concerned for her safety, Violet made sure she did not venture out in public alone, and was with Eva Morley on the day of the incident, on their way to work at the Wiltshire Bacon factory. They were walking along the 'Cinder Path' at the point where it joins Dallas Road, when Hedges approached the pair and tried to further persuade Violet to rekindle their relationship. He manhandled her, but as she struggled free and walked off, she was shot on the left side of her face, knocking out a tooth. Violet and Eva escaped to the factory and sought help. Hedges turned the gun on himself, and died later that morning in hospital. The coroner stated in his report that the infatuation and subsequent depression that Hedges suffered had led to his suicide due to an 'unbalanced' mind.[1]

Violet lost her hair due to the stress of the incident and wore a wig.[2] She went on to have a long and happy marriage, and had twin boys whilst living in Bath.

17th February 2018

An earthquake with a 4.4 magnitude on the Richter scale struck Chippenham. According to the British Geological Survey, the quake was felt over all of Wales, most of western England, east as far as London and north up to the southern edge of the Lake District. The epicentre was 20km north-east of Swansea. There were no reports of serious damage or injuries, but it was the largest earthquake to hit mainland Britain in 10 years.

Violet Collier was later happily married in Bath and went on to have twin boys. Photograph - Linda Martin (Violet's niece).

1 *Wiltshire Times*, 23 February 1929.
2 Information supplied by Linda Martin (niece of Violet Collier).

18th February 1818

Alfred Provis, Chippenham's most renowned artist, was born at Orwell House, which is now part of The Brunel pub. Alfred was the son of John Provis, timber merchant and builder, who had a library, a collection of fossils and would give lectures on many subjects including the history of Chippenham. He was an inventor and engineer but did not have much success in either field.

This oil painting is the work of Alfred Provis, dated 1867. Chippenham Museum Collection

Alfred's siblings both died young; Anne age 12 and Edwin age 17. At school it was noticed that Alfred had a talent for drawing, so John built a studio in the garden and found a tutor to teach him oil painting. Later, he left Chippenham to study under John Wood and only returned on a few brief occasions. Many of his works were exhibited in the Royal Academy. Those of the local area include a Market Place scene and an unfinished sketch of the Shambles.[1]

19th February 1944

Two airman lost their lives when the plane they were flying in over Chippenham 'dived into the ground at Englands Field' off Wood Lane. They were taking part in a training wireless telegraphy homing flight in an Airspeed Oxford I of the No 15 (Pilots) Advanced Flying Unit based at Babdown Farm in Gloucestershire.[2] The men who died were 22 year old Navigator, Flight Sergeant Trevor Evans and 20 year old Pilot, Sergeant John Thomas Brockbank. Both men were laid to rest in their native Lancashire.[3]

---

1   Daniell, pp. 213-216.
2   chippenham1939-1945.weebly.com
3   WWII, Index to Allied Airmen Roll of Honour, 1939-45.

20th February 2020

Catastrophe was narrowly avoided when the Wiltshire Air Ambulance was targeted by pranksters whilst it was flying over Chippenham. The helicopter was on the approach to land on fields at Hardenhuish school, when a bright green light filled the cockpit, shone from a laser pointer device of some kind. Although on a planned training flight, there was a serious risk to pilot safety and if it was an actual emergency, the

Wiltshire Air Ambulance began as part of a joint service in 1990. It has been stand-alone, relying on charitable donations, since 2015. Photograph - Wiltshire Air Ambulance.

helicopter would not have been able to land. Those responsible were never identified.

21st February 1854

The foundation stone of St Paul's Church was laid by Joseph Neeld, armed with a ceremonial silver trowel and mallet. An inscription was placed inside a bottle under the foundation stone along with several coins.

The architect of the building was George Gilbert Scott and it was built by Daniel Jones of Bradford on Avon. The cost of the work was met by public subscription.

A service was conducted by Rev Robert Ashe of Langley Burrell, who had donated the land. Afterwards, Mr Neeld, members of the clergy and a few of the more prominent parishioners, retired for lunch at 'The Clift', home of Charles Bailey.[1]

The population of Chippenham was around 5000 at this time, with church accommodation limited to 1000. The northern side of town was increasing in size and as part of the parish of Langley Burrell, the only church was St Peter's, which was a mile away and could only accommodate 170 worshippers. St Pauls was built as a chapel-of-ease on an acre of 'glebe' land. The cost of the build was £4000, exclusive of the tower and steeple. £1200 was raised through subscriptions.

An interesting view of St Paul's Church with the Little George public house on the left. Now one of the busiest roads in Chippenham

At the consecration on 15th April, Rev John Edward Jackson, Rector of Leigh Delamere, preached the sermon. He highlighted that it was the first church to be built in the immediate neighbourhood for 700 years. The first incumbent was Rev Thomas Augustus Strong.[2]

The tower and spire (totalling 176 feet) wasn't completed until 1860, so no bells were hanging when the church opened in 1854, with its 12-foot high tower. Lack of funds were the reason for this delay.

1   *Wiltshire Gazette*, 23 February 1854.
2   Daniell, pp.193-194.

The clock was a later addition, presented by William Henry Poynder in 1861. The first peal of eight bells were given by Fanny Colborne in the same year along with a second by Charles Bailey. Three more by Mrs Poynder in 1865 and 1875 and the remaining three were bought for £430, raised by public subscriptions in 1874 and 1875.

22nd February 1904

Miss Helen Lovell was discovered drowned in the lake at Spye Park, the seat of Captain Spicer. She had gone out for walk alone on the Monday afternoon, but when she did not return for either tea or dinner, search parties were formed. Her body was found around 8am the next day. A farewell letter was discovered in her room addressed to Lady Spicer, stating that when found, she would be dead. Captain John Spicer found the letter but thought it unimportant and destroyed it. This was an unfortunate decision as it would have removed any suspicion of foul play. The inquest found that she was 'mentally and physically weak' due

Spye Park was the seat of the Spicer family and often entertained royal visitors

to shock received because of the 'distressing circumstances' of the death of her fiancé four years earlier. She also had to undergo an operation not long after he died. A verdict of suicide was passed.[1]

1   *Weekly Mail*, 27 February 1904.

23rd February 1894

As two children played in Baydons Lane, a brick wall collapsed on top of them. The two little girls, Hester, age 6 and Eleanor, age 4, were the daughters of Charles Baker, a butcher working at the Bacon Factory. The girls were killed instantly when they were buried by the wall.[1] The incident was witnessed by their 10 year old brother Arthur.

An inquest was held at the Three Crowns, where no negligence was proven against Carrick Moore, the owner of the wall, but a recommendation was put to the town council to make a survey of walls needing attention in the area. The deepest sympathy was expressed to the parents, to which the jury donated their fees.[2]

24th February 1941

Alfred George Eyles, age 24, a married man lodging at Malmesbury Road, pleaded guilty to obtaining, by means of a trick, cigarettes and cash to the value of 14s. First he altered a halfpenny to represent a shilling, then a penny to act as a two shilling piece. Mr King, grocer of Malmesbury Road, had previously found defaced coins in his cigarette machine. Police detectives Hawkins and Rossiter kept watch until they caught Eyles in the act. Eyles told the Special Police Court that he made the coins as part of a 'silly game' even though he could afford the cigarettes. He was 'bound over' for a year and had to pay costs of £1 9s, a lenient sentence due to his clean record and previous good character.[3]

25th February 1893

Florence Hancock was born at 14 Factory Lane. Her parents, Jacob and Mary Hancock, were both weavers at Waterford Cloth Factory. Florence was one of at least 20 children, as both parents had previously been widowed, with children from those relationships as well. Despite these humble beginnings, she rose from participating in union activities at Nestlés Condensed Milk Factory, to become the Chair of the Trade Unions Congress. She was a Governor of the BBC between 1956-1962. For her contribution to society she was awarded an OBE in 1942, a CBE

---

1 *Western Mail*, 24 February 1894.
2 *Bristol Mercury*, 26 February 1894.
3 *Wiltshire Times*, 1 March 1941.

in 1947 and was made a Dame of the British Empire in 1951.[1]

26th February 1983

A ceremony took place on the occasion of Chippenham becoming twinned with La Flèche, France. The two towns had been officially united since 27th September 1982, but the agreement was signed on this day.

The idea for twinning came from a chance encounter in Kington Langley in 1980. A young Frenchman called Maxence Mulocher from La Flèche, stayed in Kington Langley whilst working for the Milk Marketing Board as part of his training as an engineer. He was introduced by the landlord of The Hit and Miss pub, to Reg and Shirley Coates who both spoke French. They were 'leading supporters of twinning for Chippenham' and soon became friends. When Maxence's parents came over to stay, they were introduced to the couple and returned to France with a good impression of Chippenham and a suggestion to their mayor that Chippenham would be a suitable twinning partner.[2]

27th February 1756

The custom of 'Throwing at Cocks on Shrove Tuesday', along with the general mistreatment of any 'feathered fowl' in the borough, was outlawed. Anyone caught abusing a bird would receive a fine of twenty shillings payable to the bailiff. The money was to be used for paying informants of such crimes and to the parish relief fund for the poor.[3]

Also known as gallicide, the custom is reputed to have originated from anti-French sentiment and was popular amongst a range of classes and age groups. The cock was a symbol of France, as the latin for both rooster and Gaul, which was the Roman name for France, was *gallus*.

An extremely cruel sport, it involved throwing sticks and stones at a cock, which was tied to a stake, until it died. By the mid-18th Century it fell out of favour with the upper classes who decided to put a stop to it.

1   CCSB 143.
2   chippenham-twinning.org.uk/la-fleche
3   Goldney.

28th February 1916

The first Exemption Tribunal was held for the Chippenham Rural District, following the introduction of conscription for war service. Present were; Mr Ralph Pearce (Chairman), Frederick Hastings Goldney, Major Cotes, Arthur Charles Kinnier, Thomas Herbert Lambert, Edmund Mainley Awdry (Clerk) and Captain Allfrey who represented the military authorities.

Giles Bullock Andrews, age 28, was granted exemption after an application by his employer, Frank Hull of Christian Malford. This was so he could continue to assist with Hull's dairy herd of 60 cows. Mr Hull also gained exemption for his foreman Herbert Butler, who was classed as being in a 'reserved occupation' and had five brothers already serving.

Other cases reviewed included; Mr Blunsdon of Castle Combe. He successfully gained exemption for his son, Albert John Blunsdon, who managed and worked the family farm. Mrs Austin, a butcher of Lacock, sought exemption for her son, Charles Edward Austin. There was buying, slaughtering and the meat round to be done and she needed both her sons for the business to continue. There was no support given for her application and exemption was refused.[1]

29th February 1936

St Mary's Roman Catholic Church opened on Station Hill. The plot of land required, had been purchased about 30 years before, but the money still had to be raised for the building work to begin. The presbytery was built first as the incumbent priest could only rent accommodation close by. The space was used for military purposes during the First World War.

This gift from Italian POWs to the people of Chippenham hangs in St Mary's Church.

1   *North Wilts Herald*, 3 March 1916.

The chapel behind, which was built in 1855, had been insufficient for the needs of the parish for a long time. It has been used as the church hall since the new church was completed. The new church could accommodate about 200 people and at the time, was needed by Catholics from Chippenham and surrounding villages as well as for those in Calne and Corsham.

All money for building was raised locally. One such fundraiser in July 1938, was an 'American Tea' and sale. This included a baby show that attracted 70 entrants. Winners were; Under 1-year, 1st Janet Knight of Downing Street and 2nd Margaret Wilson of Plantation Road; Age 1-2 years, 1st Leslie & Janet Bowd twins of Kington Langley and 2nd Barbara Case of Parliament Street; Age 2-3 years, 1st Jean Todd of Lowden and 2nd Ann Langford of The Constitutional Club.

MARCH

1st March 1938

Alderman Edward Newall Tuck shared some interesting facts about the history of the town's water supplies at the monthly town council meeting. These included the old belief that Arthur's Well (close to Bank House on Bath Road) could cure eye complaints.

Tuck had spent 'considerable time' on research, to aid with an earlier proposal to mark various historical sites of the borough. It was decided to clean and repaint the iron plate marking Monkton Spring. This used to be situated by the town bridge but is now on the wall outside the Yelde Hall. Also, plates were to be added to the house of Sir John Francis Bodinnar which was thought to be the site of

This iron plate marking Monkton Spring was originally placed close to the town bridge. It was eventually repositioned here in April 1980.

King Alfred's hunting lodge and on the Yelde Hall. The ironwork of the old Town Pump was to be re-erected in John Coles Park and Arthur's Well was to be marked due to its significance.[1]

2nd March 1943

Private Sidney Ivor Gough of the 2nd/4th Battalion King's Own Yorkshire Light Infantry, died of his wounds in Tunisia. Born in 1915, he was the son of Frederick and Elizabeth Gough of 63 Downing Street. He was an employee of Chippenham Town Council, working at John Coles Park as Assistant Park-Keeper, before commencing three years of service during the Second World War. He is buried in Medjez-El-Bab War Cemetery.[2]

3rd March 1825

At a meeting attended by a great number of Freemen of the Borough and other inhabitants, it was unanimously resolved to present petitions to both houses of Parliament, expressing the opinion that to 'grant any further concessions to the Roman Catholics would at this time be dangerous to the Protestant religion'.[3] The borough had already established itself as an opponent of the relief of Roman Catholic disabilities, with a petition signed on 22 March 1821.

4th March 1812

The Bath Coach arrived in the morning, having travelled right through the night. As was common practice at the time, three passengers were seated outside the carriage, however on this occasion, the rain had been 'violent and incessant' throughout the journey. When the coach was received, two of the men had frozen to death and the third, a soldier, was barely able to move or speak. He was put to bed after having some food and drink, but did not wake up the next day. One of the other men was identified from his papers, as being a pewterer from London. He had travelled to Bath to take the waters as a patient of Bath Hospital, having suffered from an injured wrist. He was the only one who was successfully identified and his widow later spoke highly of the kindness received by

---

1   *Wiltshire Times,* 5 March 1938.
2   chippenham1939-1945.weebly.com
3   Goldney, p.142.

the people of Chippenham. Nearly the whole town turned out for the burial of the three men, adding credit to the town's reputation.[1]

5th March 1864

A great jewel robbery took place between 2am and 3am at the premises of Mr Bullock, silversmith and jeweller, in the Market Place. Numerous gold and silver items worth between £400-£500 were stolen including many belonging to customers who had recently dropped them off to be fixed. Based on the footprints discovered, the break-in was believed to be the work of a man and a boy. Whilst trying to gain access to the back of Mr Bullock's shop, they mistakenly entered the premises of Mr Fellowes and then of Mr Quicke, a surveyor of taxes. The event was described as 'the most serious robbery ever to have occurred here'.[2] A £10 reward was offered for information leading to recovery of the items and conviction of the offenders.[3]

6th March 1891

Canon John Edward Jackson died on this day, aged 85. Jackson was born in Doncaster on 12 November 1805, the son of a banker. He was Rector of Leigh Delamere from 1845 until his death.

The grave of Canon Jackson in Leigh Delamere churchyard. Mourners had to wade through several feet of snow at his funeral.

1   *Kentish Weekly Post,* 10 March 1812.
2   *Wiltshire Gazette,* 10 March 1864.
3   *Police Gazette,* 7 March 1864.

One of the chief founders of the Wiltshire Archaeological & Natural History Society in 1853, Jackson was the first editor of their magazine and one of its first secretaries. He devoted his spare time almost exclusively to investigating the history of various parts of Wiltshire. He was described as being 'full of wit and humour, respected, upright, leading a blameless life, gentle, unassuming, modest, charitable, counsel to those in need etc'. Also a Fellow of the Society of Antiquaries, he was a 'ceaseless student and careful writer on antiquarian topics and an author of valuable works on Wiltshire archaeology and history'.[1]

When he died, he had just finished compiling the records of Longleat House for the Marquis of Bath.[2]

7th March 1946

At Chippenham Juvenile Court, four teenagers were accused of breaking and entering into the bakehouse on Wood Lane belonging to John Victor Hunt. They stole cakes with a value of 10s. The four boys, two aged 13, one 15 and one 16, all pleaded guilty. Each boy received a 5s fine, despite one of the fathers pleading their case, arguing that they were tempted when they saw an easy way in and were more mischievous than criminal. The court chairman suggested that the boys would benefit from joining a juvenile organisation to keep them out of trouble and reminded the parents that it was their job to discipline them.[3]

8th March 1946

An RAF Gloster Meteor on a routine training flight, crashed at Kellaways.

The plane ploughed through a coppice of trees, crossed a road and field for 300 yards, pulled down telephone wires and then exploded, scattering the wreckage. Described by eyewitnesses as a mock attack on a train, it reached a 'terrific speed', and narrowly missed several houses.

Pilot Officer Dinshaw Sorab Bamjee was thrown out of the cockpit and killed instantly. A member of the Royal Indian Air Force, he

1   WFHS, p 27.
2   *North Wilts Herald,* 13 March 1891.
3   *Western Gazette,* 8 March 1946.

RAF Hullavington, 1947. A Gloster Meteor similar to the one which crashed at Kellaways a year earlier.

was attached to the 74th Squadron based at RAF Colerne.[1] He is commemorated on the Air Forces Memorial at Runnymede in Surrey, along with all RAF personnel who have no known grave. Bamjee was 23 and from Streatham, London were he lived with his wife Joyce.[2]

9th March 1974

It was the 25th Anniversary Dinner for the Chippenham Soroptimist Club at the town hall. This was the 'daughter branch' of the Bath Soroptimist Club and was founded in 1948, one of four new clubs to join the divisional union extending from Wiltshire and Gloucester to Plymouth, in that year.

1   *Western Daily Press*, 9 March 1946.
2   Andrews Newspaper Index Cards, 1790-1976.

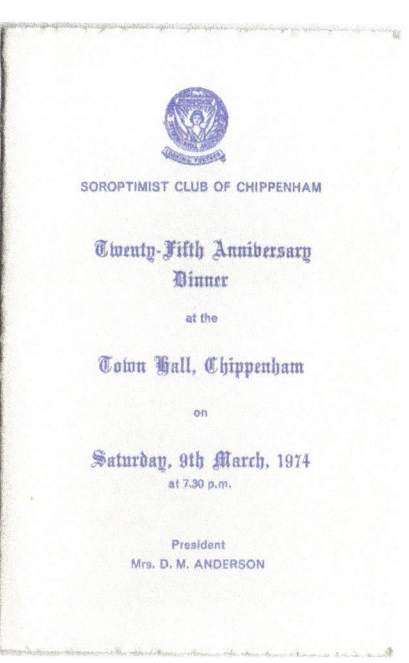

Front cover of the menu from the Soroptimist Club's 25th Anniversary Dinner

The name Soroptimist comes from the Latin 'soror' meaning sister, and 'optima' meaning best. Soroptimist therefore means 'the best for women'.[1]

10th March 1893

At Warrilow's gun factory, a lad named Frederick William Hampton was filling cartridges when he placed a can containing a couple of pounds of powder inside it on a stove. The powder had become 'clotty' and wouldn't go into the holes on the filling machine, so he hoped it would dry out using this method. Instead it exploded and it was extremely fortunate no one got caught in the blast.[2]

Proceedings were taken against both Hampton and his employer, James Bakewell Warrilow, under the Explosives Act of 1875. Both received fines. William Hampton is recorded on the 1891 census living at Westmead Lane, aged 15. His occupation is listed as 'cartridge filler at gun works', so it appears he wasn't inexperienced when the incident occurred. His father, Henry Hampton, was manager of the gasworks which was where the family lived.

11th March 1989

The first birth took place at the newly opened Greenways Maternity Unit at St Andrew's Hospital. The baby, Emma Naomi Pardoe, weighed 8lbs 1oz and was baby number two for Mother Jane Pardoe, age 30 of Minster Way. Mrs Pardoe's first child was born at the original Greenways off Malmesbury Road.[3]

The £205,000 move to St Andrew's Hospital was part of a long term strategy to bring

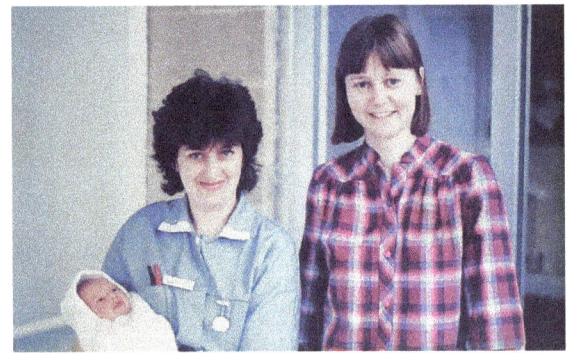

Baby Emma with Midwife Christine Berry and Mum Jane Pardoe. Photograph - Emma Hildebrandt

1   soroptimistinternational.org/about-us/history/
2   *Evening Express,* 10 March 1893.
3   *Gazette & Herald,* 16 March 1989.

all facilities to one site.¹ This plan included the closure of hospitals at Frogwell and London Road.

Three mothers and their babies were transferred from Greenways to the new 10-bed unit when it opened. The League of Friends presented two framed pictures of Greenways and a pewter cup to be given to the first baby.²

12th March 1981

It was the opening night of Goldiggers nightclub. Nigel Ross, at the age of just 19, became Britain's youngest nightclub owner. Fellow directors were brother David, father Gilbert and Bruce Bronson. The Ross family were already well known in the town, due to their work in the west country motor trade.

Astrid Broderstad, otherwise known as 'Miss Thamesdown', was at the opening along with nearly 600 guests.

The first star booking was comedian Tommy Cooper two days later. Other acts secured in the early days included Hot Gossip, Showaddywaddy, Canon & Ball, Slade, Ken Dodd, Little & Large and The Wurzels.

Goldiggers Exhibition at Chippenham Museum, February 2020

Goldiggers went on to become one of the premier venues in the west country for 25 years. The nightclub was created inside the former Classic Cinema building in Timber Street, which was originally opened as part of the Gaumont chain in 1936. Renovations cost c£150,000.

1   *Wiltshire Times*, 12 May 1989.
2   *Gazette & Herald*, 16 March 1989.

The Buttercross, May 2022. Re-erected by Chippenham Civic Society in 1995

13th March 1995

This date marked the completion of the first stage of traffic alterations giving pedestrians priority in the town centre. This also enabled the re-erection of the Buttercross, as the road in front of the Angel Hotel was closed to traffic. A new oak roof was in position on May Day with a sprig of oak attached to its apex. This is a centuries old tradition that signifies the completion of an oak framework. The replanting of trees was also part of this project, with 144 oak saplings set to be planted at Mortimores Wood.

14th March 2020

The impact of the Coronavirus, or COVID-19, was now beginning to effect everyday life in Chippenham, only three days after the World Health Organisation declared a pandemic. In America, President Donald Trump declared a state of emergency. Panic buying was well under way in the UK leading to shortages in food, sanitiser and toilet paper.

This day was the last Saturday before restrictions on large gatherings and events in the UK. Chippenham Town and Wealdstone drew 1-1 at

Hardenhuish Park in what was to be the last game of the 2019/2020 season. Chippenham Park Run in Monkton Park held its last event until 24 July 2021.

Four days later Prime Minster Boris Johnson ordered that all schools should shut indefinitely and on 23 March the first national lockdown began.

Panic buying led to empty shelves at Sainsbury's Chippenham, March 2020.

15th March 1916

Alderman John Coles passed away aged 73. He was a man 'who put his heart into everything appertaining to the benefit of the town'

John Coles. Photograph - Janice Robinson

and almost in his last conscious moments, wished to discuss the work of the council who knew him as their 'Chancellor of the Exchequer'.

Coles became a councillor in 1886 and was mayor three times. He had also been the Chairman of the Finance Committee since 1889. He was 'intimately associated with the counsels of the Liberal Party' in Chippenham. His greatest public work was the 'initiating, financing and building' of Chippenham & District Technical School at Cocklebury Road, where he was Chairman of Governors. Coles was also recognised as a distinguished public speaker.[1]

1   *Wiltshire Times,* 8 April 1916.

He lived in the Market Place where he traded as Chemist, Grocer, and Wine and Spirit Merchant.

Coles left an estate of around £10,000, of which £4,000 was bequeathed to the Mayor and Corporation of Chippenham, to use for the benefit of the people of the town for 'some scheme which would be for the welfare of the human being by promoting the health of the body and the recreation and improvement of the mind', allowing them their own unfettered choice. This money was used to pay for the land which later became John Coles Park.[1]

16th March 1858

Charles Spurgeon, the famous Baptist preacher, visited Chippenham. He delivered two sermons at the cheese market where approximately 3,000 people were in attendance. The anticipation to his arrival in the town was fuelled when he missed his train from Paddington and didn't arrive until 3pm. Spurgeon's 'full and hearty voice' filled the whole market.

There was a collection held on behalf of the New Baptist Chapel. Many of the local ministers put £300 towards the cost of the building on Station Hill. Spurgeon hoped to relieve some of this burden. The collections for both services amounted to about £70.[2]

17th March 1869

A sensation was caused by the sudden closure of Rowland Brotherhood's railway works and dismissal of all 200 of his employees. Although the state of the business was not a secret and the closure not totally unexpected, it was hoped that the large contract Brotherhood had secured with the Brazilian Government, would improve the situation. He called all his employees together, promised they would receive all wages due to them and then declared himself 'a ruined man for life'.[3]

Brotherhood came to Chippenham 'a poor but hardworking, industrious, enterprising man' in 1842, managed to achieve personal worth of £100,000, but left the town 'a father of a dozen children, with

1 *Wiltshire Times,* 13 May 1916.
2 *Wiltshire Gazette,* 18 March 1858.
3 *Wiltshire Gazette,* 18 March 1869.

Landsend Place was built by Rowland Brotherhood in 1854

scarcely a penny in his pocket'.[1]

Brotherhood had contributed significantly to the prosperity of Chippenham when his business was thriving. As well as being a large employer, he also built housing for some of his workers at Landsend Place on Marshfield Road, in 1854.

In January 1872 he took up management of Bute Ironworks in Cardiff.

Still empty in 1883, the old factory at Foundry Lane was acquired by Evans O'Donnell and later by Saxby & Farmer, signal manufacturers. Brotherhood died on 4th March of the same year, at his home in Redland, Bristol. He was buried at Arnos Vale Cemetery, where there is a fine monument marking his grave.

18th March 1913

Canon John Rich died at his home, Lowden Lodge on Lowden Hill, aged 87. He was the eldest son of the Reverend John Rich, vicar of Ivinghoe, Buckinghamshire.

Lowden Lodge, Lowden Hill. This house used to be a vicarage.

1   *The Industrial Railway Record*, April 1969.

During his early years he was a pupil at Westminster School, which gave him the opportunity to attend Queen Victoria's Coronation at the Abbey.[1] Between 1844 and 1862, he was a mathematics student at Christ Church, Oxford and in the spring of 1860, was photographed by Lewis Carroll.

His funeral took place at Tytherton Churchyard after a service at St Andrew's, where there was a large attendance including the Mayor Alderman Edgar Neale, Sir Audley Dallas Neeld and Sir Prior Goldney. Rich was 'beloved and respected by everyone' and was best known in Chippenham for his 44 years service as vicar of St Andrew's. On his retirement in 1904, he was given the Rectorship of Kellaways by Sir Audley Neeld, his last service taking place only a couple of weeks before his death.[2]

19th March 2012

A tabby and tortoiseshell coloured cat was discovered tied up in a pillow case and dumped down a drain in Larkham Rise, off London Road. Fortunately, a passerby heard its cries and alerted the RSPCA. Their inspector rescued the adult female from about three feet down in the drain. It was unhurt and in good condition, but unsurprisingly traumatised. The drain was dry, but if it had rained, the cat would have most likely drowned.[3]

20th March 2000

Chippenham Museum & Heritage Centre opened in its new home at 10-11 Market Place, after 36 years at the Yelde hall. Project Officer Anne Lineen 'worked tirelessly' on the launch from June 1999. Lottery funding was not forthcoming so Chippenham Town Council stepped in to help with the cost of the relocation. The museum initially started with four galleries on the ground floor only.

21st March 1941

William Upton, described by Superintendent Sadler as a 'quarrelsome pest', was sent to prison for 14 days for assaulting a

1   *The Times*, 19 March 1913.
2   *North Wilts Herald*, 21 March 1913
3   bbc.co.uk/news/uk-england-wiltshire

police constable. Police War Reserve Martin was cycling along Wood Lane when he saw Upton's nine year old son hit another boy with a stone from a catapult. Martin confiscated the catapult but soon the boy's father was on the scene and a tussle ensued resulting in Martin becoming injured.[1]

The Police War Reserve Constable (WRC), also known as a War Reserve Police Constable (WRPC), was a voluntary role during war time. They were sworn in under the Special Constables Act 1923, with the full powers of a regular police constable.

22nd March 1934

William Wheeler was delivering firewood on his round at Tugela Road when his pony recognised the van from Hale's bakery. Wheeler, of the Causeway, would stop at the baker's shop each morning for some 'Lardy', a traditional Wiltshire delicacy, and the pony would have a nibble.

On this particular occasion the pony was left unattended, as was Hale's van, so he took his chance. He opened the doors at the back by turning the handle and was discovered by the driver, head and shoulders inside rooting for a treat. After shutting the doors and making another call further along his journey, once unattended again, the pony went back and repeated his trick![2]

23rd March 1867

A combination of melting snow and heavy rain led to the worst flood in the town for 40 years. By the time the water had reached its greatest height, many had to abandon the lower floors of their homes, with considerable damage to property. Smaller livestock such as pigs and chickens were swept away never to be seen again. When the bridge became impassable to pedestrians, a few 'enterprising parties' offered safe passage with their own vehicles, for a small sum of course! At one point, the Foghamshire area was under several feet of water.[3]

1 *Wiltshire Times*, 19 April 1941.
2 *North Wilts Herald*, 29 March 1934.
3 *Wiltshire Times*, 30 March 1867.

24th March 1930

It was the last meeting of the Board of Guardians, their work from then on being the responsibility of the county council. The House Committee gave thanks for the many years service of the Chairman, Henry Robert Beauclerk Coventry. As an item of interest, he produced the record of the first Guardians meeting on 3rd December 1835. As the meeting ended, the members were photographed in front of the institution.[1]

25th March 1929

The sudden death of respected publican George William Bensley, brought sadness to the town on this day. Bensley was landlord of the Black Horse on New Road for almost 21 years. He was attending a meeting of the North West Wiltshire Licensed Victualler's Association at

The Black Horse c1913. Landlord George William Bensley (right) and son Arthur George Bensley (centre) are pictured with an unidentified individual. Photograph - Simon Bensley

the Lansdowne Arms Hotel in Calne. Near the end of the meeting, having just stood to make a motion proposing a grant from the Benevolent Fund, he suddenly fell forwards into his chair and passed away. Jack

1   *North Wilts Herald*, 28 March 1930.

Walters, landlord of the Railway Inn, rushed back to Chippenham to inform the widow and a doctor, who subsequently confirmed the cause of death was due to the heart trouble that Bensley had been suffering from since Christmas.

Bensley was an ex-Royal Marine Sergeant, originally from East Anglia and was 63 when he died. Twice married, he left a son by his first wife, who was living in India. Bensley came to Chippenham around 32 years previously on his appointment as steward of the Constitutional Club. He was then landlord of the Royal Oak on London Road until 1907 when he took over at the Black Horse.[1]

26th March 1899

The Great Western Railway company began making extensive alterations to the station at Chippenham. The platforms were widened to double the previous width and the large roof which used to cover the station was removed and replaced by a verandah on each platform. This had already been carried out at Bath in a similar way. Waiting and refreshment rooms on the 'upside' were pulled down and rebuilt on a larger scale. The booking office was also altered on the other platform. The work was carried out by Messrs Pattison & Sons of London, who had just completed changes to the station at Reading.

27th March 1955

The Chippenham Sea Cadets moved to their new home off Long Close at the old bathing place on a bend in the River Avon. The new premises became known as TS Tiger.

The former swimming changing rooms there were adapted for use as classrooms, and a mast was placed on the 'bridge', which had came from a ship docked in Southampton. For the previous ten years the group had used an old war-time hutted camp called TS Cyclops, at Cocklebury.

On the day, the signal to 'Abandon Ship' was made and the entire Sea Cadet unit manned their fleet of a cutter, whaler and dinghies, with Commanding Officer Lieutenant Jack Cohu leading, and took to the river. On arrival the cadets were greeted by Mayor and Mayoress Vince and many others including parents, friends and well-wishers.[2]

1 *Wiltshire Times*, 30 March 1929.
2 *Wiltshire Times*, 2 April 1955.

28th March 1933

A curious incident occurred at the point where Foghamshire meets New Road and the bottom of Monkton Hill. Just after a large lorry passed the spot, a three-foot wide hole appeared in the centre of the road. A crust of Tarmac two inches thick was left, but below it was a 'yawning cavern' approximately ten feet deep and large enough to fit two small cars. The cause was believed to be a defect in the storm overflow sewer and the subsequent continual swirling of flood and storm water in a giant whirlpool underground. Fortunately no one was hurt.[1] This phenomenon is known as a sinkhole.

29th March 1949

There was a strike by 100 employees of Bulwark Transport Company in Wood Lane. This delayed approximately 40,000 gallons of milk that should have been transported to London during the night. The men were protesting against one of their colleagues being given notice to leave, however the strike was unofficial and against the advice of their union.[2]

A Bulwark tanker. Postcard - Paula Champion

1   *Wiltshire Times*, 1 April 1933.
2   *The Times*, 30 March 1949.

The company was originally set up in 1934 and by 1937 had a fleet of 17 tankers transporting the majority of locally produced milk. By 1952 this had grown to 130, transporting a variety of liquids for many large companies.[1]

Bulwark left the town in 1984 after they were approached by CH Beazer who wanted to purchase the yard in order to build 104 new homes. This wasn't without controversy as there was concern that chemicals may not have been correctly removed from the site.[2]

30th March 1877

A 'horrific incident' took place on Good Friday, involving Louisa Hart, servant to Thomas Holloway, a gunmaker. Thomas answered her cries for help, finding her on fire with flames reaching to the ceiling. She ran into the garden where they were joined by PC Myall, who heard the commotion and extinguished the fire whilst Thomas quickly secured his gunpowder store.

It appears that Louisa had been filling a lamp with Benzoline, and dropped the bottle next to the gunpowder store. Wiping it up whilst using a small lamp so she could see, she accidentally dropped it onto the oil. It took about a minute to extinguish the flames, by which time she was completely burned apart from her face and parts of her neck and chest. Louisa later died due to her horrific injuries.[3] She was only 15.

Thomas Holloway of Cook Street, originally from York, was recorded as a land surveyor on all records, so his gun making must have been a sideline. There are, however, examples of his work still in existence today.

31st March 1868

An inquest was held at the Great Western Hotel into the circumstances of the sudden death of Sarah Coombs, a widow of Providence Place. She was discovered lying on her back with ashes and coal scattered around her. Mr Stiles, surgeon, confirmed that her death was not suspicious and from natural causes, probably heart disease. The foreman stated that the jury felt Coombs shouldn't have been living alone considering her health problems, but Dr Charles Bailey said that he

1   rrtha.org.uk
2   *Bristol Evening Post*, 25 September 1984.
3   *Swindon Advertiser*, 9 April 1877.

had tried to place a married couple in the house with her. Mrs Coombs had became quite angry when it was suggested.[1]

Providence Place was a terrace of six houses in Foghamshire, but is not to be confused with Providence Terrace which still stands in front of Ivy Lane School. It was occupied solely by widows of 'medical gentlemen', rent free. The eccentric surgeon, Charles Bailey of the Clift, built the terrace in 1855 as part of his work for the Medical Benevolent Trust.[2]

The Great Western Hotel was demolished in 1966 for a 'relief road' linking Marshfield Road and Ivy Lane.

APRIL

1st April 1950

A huge event that took place on this date, was the funeral of popular fishmonger Joseph Henry 'Joe' Buckle, who died age 76 on 27 March. For many years he had served the community as the captain of Chippenham Fire Brigade. He became part of public life in the town through serving on the town council, and as secretary of the swimming club and also as part of the Lansdowne Lodge of Freemasons.[3]

Around 50 firemen were present at the funeral, some of whom carried the coffin, which was draped in a Union Flag, topped by Buckle's own fire helmet. Numerous representatives from organisations with which Buckle was part of, or linked to, were at the service.

On news of his death, the family were sent a letter of condolence from Queen Mary's Comptroller.[4] Buckle's impressive collection of fire marks were admired by Queen Mary in a visit to his shop whilst she stayed at Badminton.

2nd April 1949

It was the closing day of the Westinghouse Exhibition in the Neeld Hall. Over 16,000 people from across the country and abroad had attended.

One of the highlights for visitors was the opportunity to test out

1 *Western Daily Press*, 2 April 1868.
2 Platts, p.68.
3 *Wiltshire Times & Trowbridge Advertiser*, 3 January 1925.
4 *Western Daily Press*, 3 April 1950.

train announcement recording equipment, which was hoped to become adaptable for making talking books for the blind.¹

3rd April 1989

The leader of the Social and Liberal Democrat Party, Paddy Ashdown, visited Chippenham to support local Democrat candidates for the county elections. These were; June Wood (Sheldon), Steve Spear (Chippenham Town) and Patrick Coleman (Chippenham Park).² All three were successful on 4th May, as the Liberal Democrat Party held control of the town.

Steve Spear, June Wood and Patrick Coleman celebrate election victory a month after Paddy Ashdown's visit to Chippenham. Photograph - Steve Spear.

4th April 1950

Arthur Hull, whilst driving a Co-operative Society van, collided with the milestone close to the Plough Inn at Kington Langley.

The van mounted the verge and came to rest on top of the stone. Mr Hull and his passenger Mrs Williams were both thrown from the vehicle into a ditch. Both were in shock but un-injured.³

Arthur Albert Hull, of The Barton, Kington Langley, was listed as a bakery bread distributor on the 1939 Register.

5th April 1894

A mysterious suicide occurred on the Great Western Railway. The 'Flying Dutchman' was

Milestone at Kington Langley on the old Malmesbury Road behind The Plough

1   *Wiltshire Times*, 9 April 1949.
2   *Wiltshire Times*, 7 April 1989.
3   *Wiltshire Times*, 8 April 1950.

travelling between Swindon and Chippenham at 50mph, when a man jumped from a third-class carriage. After landing and breaking his leg, he then cut his throat. The smartly dressed man was identified by his papers and clothing, as an artist named Charles Harbord Morant.[1]

6th April 1858

On this day St Paul's School was formally opened.[2] It was built on the site of a former 'dame school' established on pasture land known as 'Home Ground' or sometimes 'Brook Ground'. This land, worth £200 at the time, was given by the Rev Robert Martin Ashe on 12 January 1857. The school buildings were the work of Mr Weaver, an architect from Devizes.

7th April 2013

The popular Chas Hart Jewellers closed for the last time. The business was acquired by John Knight in 1965 and continued after his death a decade later, by his wife Anne, later joined by their two children. Originally on the high street, the business moved into the Market Place

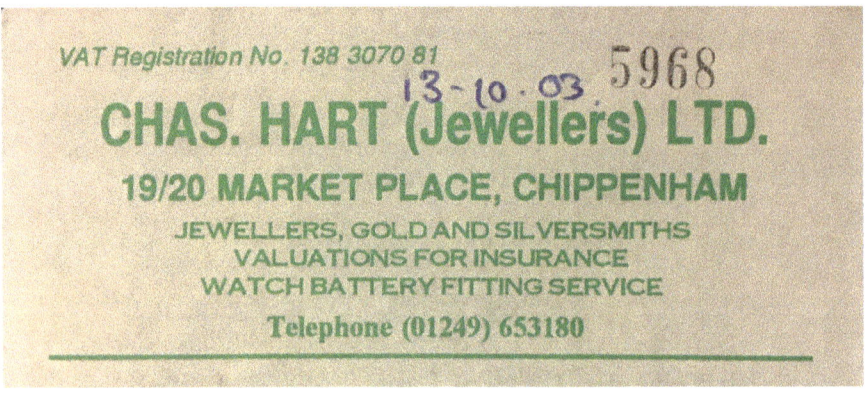

Receipt head from Chas Hart jewellers

shop, which was formerly Heath's Stationers, in 1984. The shop was a specialist in second hand jewellery. The building is now occupied by an electronic-cigarette retailer.[3]

1   *The Pall Mall Gazette*, 6 April 1894.
2   *Devizes and Wiltshire Gazette*, 15 April 1858.
3   *Gazette & Herald*, 4 April 2013.

A triple wedding at St Paul's Church in 1939. John Summers stands proudly with six of his daughters. Chippenham Museum Collection

8th April 1939

There was a rare triple wedding at St Paul's Church. Laura, Aline and Mildred Summers, the third, fourth and fifth daughters of John Summers of Cocklebury Farm Cottages, were the brides. Three other daughters, Ruby, Ivy and Peggy were bridesmaids and the seventh daughter lent her own wedding veil. The bridegrooms were William Whale, Bert Golding and Oliver Baker. Mr Whale and Mr Baker were cousins. A brother, Charles Summers, was a best man.[1]

9th April 1952

The Rotary club launched a public appeal for the collection of household items as part of their 'Aid for Greece' campaign, at a meeting led by the Mayor. The country was still recovering from the effects of war and those present were reminded that Greece was Britain's only ally for a time after Dunkirk. The Greek people ensured no British troops were captured by the Germans and because of that, suffered retaliation by the burning down of 800 villages. It was felt that it was

1   *Shepton Mallet Journal*, 14 April 1939.

only right to repay their people with aid.[1]

British aid to Greece had ended in 1947 due to this country's own financial difficulties and the fact that the US had began to financially support the country as part of the Marshall Plan.

10th April 1979

The world railway service speed record was set by a British Railways Inter-City 125 train. It was achieved by the 09.20 service from London Paddington to Bristol with 300 passengers on board. A distance of 94 miles to Chippenham was covered in 50 minutes and 31 seconds with an average speed of 111.7mph, which was 5mph faster than the previous world record set in Japan.

11th April 1895

A fatal accident occurred at the Signal and Engineering Works. Edwin Cleaver was killed when the 'emery wheel' he was working at broke into three pieces, one of which struck him on the neck.[2] The wheel was spinning at around 2000 rpm. A rest across the wheel may

Employees of Saxby & Farmer. Postcard - Paula Champion

1   *Wiltshire Times*, 5 April 1952.
2   *Morning Post*, 12 April 1895.

have helped prevent the death, but Cleaver would say he 'worked better without it'.

Cleaver lived at Foundry Lane but was born in Tetbury. He was buried at St Paul's Church on 15th April, leaving a widow but no children. The 36 year old was described as a 'first-rate workman' by Percy Baylis, Managing Director.[1]

12th April 1935

A Labour Hall opened opposite the railway station on Cocklebury Road. The Rt. Hon. George Lansbury MP, who was the leader of the Labour Party at the time, officiated.[2] He was also the grandfather of actress Angela Lansbury of 'Murder, She Wrote' fame.

The hall became the Post Office Sports & Social Club, when it reopened in 1978 after a period of neglect. This became known as the 'Buzby Club' after the yellow cartoon bird used in BT advertising. It is now called The Cocklebury Club.

Left to right: Jack Sunderland, Arnie Highmore, Trevor Williamson, Dave Newth, Ron Ayres, Mick Hyde

The Cocklebury Club on the occasion of its reopening in December 1978. Photograph - Paul Stephens

13th April 1927

A presentation was made to William George Bryant upon his retirement from Westmead School, as headmaster there for over 40 years since January 1887. Bryant received a wallet with £15 and an album of 400 names all wishing to express their gratitude for his service. He acknowledged his wife's support, having only had two weeks off in the whole 40 years! He estimated that around 2,500 children had passed through the school during his time, and also wished to highlight that 40 former pupils sacrificed their lives for the country during the war. He announced that he and his wife were

1 *Wiltshire Times*, 20 April 1895.
2 *North Wilts Herald*, 18 April 1935.

Westmead School, 1932. Photograph - Jean Morrison

leaving the town to live in Weymouth, for the benefit of Mrs Bryant's health.[1]

14th April 1987

The new Southern Ambulance Training School was opened by Baroness Trumpington, Parliamentary Undersecretary of State at the DHSS. The Mayor, Michael May and his wife Barbara, were also present. The new facility situated on Malmesbury Road, cost £1.5million. When opened it was only the second of its kind in the country with state of the art training equipment and facilities.

A mock emergency was carried out to

Southern Ambulance Training School, 1988. Photograph - Bill Lynch

1   *Wiltshire Times*, 16 April 1927.

demonstrate some of the training the students were receiving.

Tamsin Delahaye, age 11, of Wyndham Close, presented a basket of flowers to the baroness once the plaque was unveiled and the opening was made official.[1] Tamsin's father was a paramedic trainer at the school. She remembers being very nervous at the time![2]

15th April 1912

Two residents of Chippenham, Thomas Henry Davison and his wife Mary, were passengers on the ill-fated maiden voyage of the RMS Titanic. Born in 1880, Thomas (known as Harry) was the blacksmith

RMS Titanic leaving Southampton on 10 April 1912. Photographer - Francis Godolphin Osbourne Stuart (1843-1923). Photo in the public domain.

son of Thomas Cook Henry Davison, a corn miller, and Sarah Ann Long of Sheldon Road. He was living at Woodlands Road when he married Mary Elizabeth Finkenagel of Malmesbury in 1902. After, the couple resided at 32 Marshfield Road following a brief stay in Cleveland, Ohio

1 *Wiltshire Times* & *News*, 17 April 1987.
2 Memory of Tamsin Delahaye, November 2020.

in 1908, which was where Mary's family were from. They decided to return to America to settle in Bedford, Ohio, but postponed their departure so they could 'enjoy the novelty' of crossing on the famous ship. They bought 3rd Class tickets in 'steerage' for £16 2s and boarded at Southampton on 10 April 1912.

Thomas was woken when the ship hit the iceberg, dressed to see what had happened, then returned to wake his wife. She survived, but Thomas was lost, his body never found or identified.

16th April 1869

The toll collector for the Langley Burrell turnpike, William Mitchell, demanded an excessive toll from Stephen Smart, who was on route to Sutton Benger from Chippenham. All other tolls run by the same turnpike trust had charged him 3d, but Mitchell would not let Smart pass until 4d was paid up. Mitchell was later summoned to court by Smart, where he was fined 1s and 12s costs for his action.[1]

17th April 1960

American rock 'n roll singer Eddie Cochran tragically died age 21, the day after the taxi he was travelling in crashed into a lamppost on Rowden Hill. Cochran was travelling to London after finishing his British tour so he could fly back to America and had been top of the bill at the 'Big Beat Show' held at the Bristol Hippodrome. He was with fellow star Gene Vincent, Patrick Tompkins their tour manager, and his songwriter girlfriend Sharon Sheeley.

The improved Eddie Cochran memorial on Rowden Hill.

The car, a cream coloured Consul, spun in the road after a tyre burst, and collided backwards into the lamppost, throwing all the passengers out. Cochran sustained severe head injuries. The driver, George Martin of Hartcliffe in Bristol, was unhurt.

1   *North Wilts Herald*, 15 May 1869

Cochran was famous for his hits 'Summertime Blues', 'C'mon Everybody' and 'Three Steps to Heaven' which was released on schedule only a few days after his death.

18th April 1772

Economist David Ricardo was born on this day. Ricardo's ideas were highly influential on the development of economics and he is often ranked as the second most important economic thinker behind Adam Smith. He died at Gatcombe Park, Gloucestershire on 11th September 1823 and is buried at St Nicholas Church, Hardenhuish.

Ricardo Memorial, Hardenhuish Church

19th April 1899

An inquest into the death of William Chivers of Foghamshire took place at the Temperance Hall there. William, who had been a shunter on the Great Western Railway for 33 years, had complained of chest pains but did not go to the doctor. The morning of his death, his daughter Caroline Chivers, took him some water and washed his face as he was feeling giddy, but then he died in her arms.

Dr Wilson visited three months earlier as William was suffering from influenza and gout, which he believed, may have not entirely gone away.

The inquest found the cause of death to be 'syncope[1] caused by suppressed gout'.[2]

---

1 Syncope is a medical term for fainting or passing out.
2 *Bristol Mercury*, 21 April 1899.

20th April 1915

On this day, 20-year old volunteer soldier Joseph Stanley Victor Fox, known as Victor, was shot for desertion at Ypres, Belgium. Fox was born in Corsham but lived at 45 Causeway. He was a Lance Corporal in 1st Battalion Wiltshire Regiment, but was attached to 3rd Division Cyclist Company when he deserted. His parents, Charles and Harriet Fox, also of 45 Causeway, did not receive confirmation of their son's death from the War Office, but instead from a fellow soldier who knew Victor. Charles soon joined up to avenge his death.

Victor is listed on the war memorial in Market Place, not common of those 'shot at dawn'. An error, whether deliberate or otherwise, meant that nobody found out the truth about his death and he was commemorated, as he should have been, as another brave victim of war.[1]

Tragedy had previously befallen the family in March 1909 when Victor's younger brother, Sidney Herbert Fox, drowned when he fell from the Back Avon Bridge whilst walking home from Ivy Lane School. He was only five years old. The water level was almost the same height as the bridge, which would have been swollen by recent heavy rains.

Charles Fox was a local manager for billposter company Messrs Billing, Jarrett & Read Co. He had 16 children to provide for. The family later moved to Warminster.

21st April 1785

Less than two years after the first manned balloon flight took place in Paris on 21st November 1783, Chippenham residents were amazed by the appearance of a hot air balloon over their town.

The 'incomparable grand and majestic gold and silver air balloon' was 25 feet in diameter, with an ornate car to seat the pilot and oars for 'steering.'

The pilot was 18 year old, Joseph Deeker, taking off from Bristol at 3.45pm. The strong wind enabled the balloon to cover the 26 miles to Chippenham in only 32 minutes. It landed 2 and a half miles east of the town, where Deeker was met by a 'great concourse of people who conducted him to Chippenham on horseback with acclamation of joy'. The wind had kept him so low at times, that he had to dispose of all his

1   pro-patria.co.uk

ballast (including his boots and bottle of brandy!) to free himself from trees and hedges.[12]

22nd April 1848

The Wilts & Dorset Bank in Chippenham was robbed of £7,000 in notes and coinage. The manager at the time was Mr Broome Pinniger.[3] This was the third such robbery on a branch of the Wilts & Dorset Bank in eighteen months.[4] It was believed that a skeleton key was used to gain access. A £200 reward was offered to catch those responsible.[5]

23rd April 1932

Around 1.30pm, Stanley Hemmings of Rowden Place, was cycling along Bath Road on his way back to work after lunch, when he heard a women crying for help from across the fields. What he discovered was an extreme act of heroism and endurance from a 23 year old domestic servant. Hemmings found the woman knee deep in the brook holding the head of an unconscious man above the water.

The man was Cecil King, age 35, a farmer living with his parents at Derriads Farm and the young women was Marion Chaffey, his partner of two years.

It seems that Cecil acted out of character by asking Marion to jump into the stream with him. When she refused, he jumped in alone. Marion then went in after him and held him up out of the water for an estimated three hours.[6]

24th April 1805

The turnpike trustees were granted permission to erect a toll gate on the town bridge.[7] Evidence of this has long gone but other signs of the turnpike network can still be seen in the area. Toll houses stand proudly at Lowden Hill, Bristol Road and London Road at the turning

1   *The Times*, 22 April 1785.
2   Penny, p.6.
3   *Wiltshire Gazette*, 18 May 1848.
4   *Glasgow Courier*, 29 April 1848.
5   *The Sun* (London), 26 April 1848.
6   *Wiltshire Times*, 30 April 1932.
7   Chamberlain, J.A., (1976), p.21.

Toll house on the corner of Stanley Lane and London Road

for Abbeyfield School. Also, a few milestones are still in situ, such as on Malmesbury Road and Bath Road.

25th April 1942

Chippenham made preparations for air raids at the start of the Second World War and German aerial photographs prove that it was an intended target. Along with private Anderson shelters in gardens, public air raid shelters were provided at The Wharf, the town hall arches and at the cattle market (each with accommodation for 50), and in a section of the Ivy Lane railway arch (with accommodation for 115).[1]

In February 1941, sandbags were delivered to every house in Chippenham as a precaution for possible fire bomb raids. Volunteers shifted 40 tons of sand to 3750 homes, with local builders lending their lorries free of charge.

There was only one raid on Chippenham, with bombs dropped at the Folly in Bristol Road. During a raid by enemy aircraft on Bath, a German plane carried out a 'dive bombing attack'. Frederick and Ada Bowden were killed, two people hospitalised and others received minor injuries. Four bombs were dropped, three of them running in a line diagonally across the gardens of a row of houses. The fourth scored a direct hit on Firlands, the home of the Bowden family. Frederick, a retired railwayman had gone upstairs and his wife was seated in a downstairs room with their daughter,

1   *Wiltshire Times*, 6 July 1940.

a secondary school teacher. The house was completely destroyed except for the chimney stack, their daughter's escape was described as 'miraculous'. She was blown out of the house by the blast and was found walking in the road by the ARP who had rushed to the scene. Her parents bodies were recovered from the wrecked building a couple of hours later.[1]

Julie Townsend's uncle was thrown from the back door into his garden at Bristol Road.[2] A mile and a half away at Patterdown, a big crack appeared on the landing of the house of the Jones family, such was the force of the blasts.[3]

The grave of Frederick and Ada Bowden at Hardenhuish, close to the Ricardo tomb

26th April 1879

John Butler and Isaac Humphries, heading a gang of men from Lacock, were on Bath Road when they set upon Henry Dyke and Alfred Beard. Dyke, of Lowden and Beard, of Corsham, were both badly beaten. There was no clear motive. At the Petty Sessions the men were warned not to get into bother again. Both Butler and Humphries were ordered to pay fines and costs.[4]

27th April 1860

A 'painful and extraordinary sensation' gripped the town by the news of the 'mysterious and frightful' death of William Gale, age 62. The previous day, a Friday, had been a rather successful market day for Gale. He was a farmer who held a considerable amount of land at Horton near Badminton in Gloucestershire. He spent the evening drinking freely in the Great Western Hotel and left on horseback in an intoxicated state. He had only rode half a mile before he was either thrown from the horse or fell off.

In the early hours, an elderly woman found Gale marked with blood

1   *Wiltshire Times*, 2 May 1942.
2   Julie Townsend, CSN.
3   Marian Jones, CSN.
4   *Bristol Mercury*, 3 May 1879.

and clearly dead. Bizarrely, his horse was later found wandering in the Corsham area.[1]

28th April 1962

This day marked the last game played by Chippenham United Football Club. United lost 0-3 to Devizes Town. Financial problems caused by falling attendances were given as the main cause of the club's demise. The home ground of The Firs at Hungerdown Lane was later used for housing, but a line of fir trees still exist, showing where the edge of the ground used to be.

The day before the match, an announcement was made that 'public apathy had beaten Chippenham United'. No decision on the future of the club was actually made at that time, but no competitions were entered for the next season. As well as falling attendances, support for 'live saving fund raising schemes' also decreased. Some hoped for a merger with Chippenham Town FC, but this wasn't to be. By the 12 September, a change of use application was passed for The Firs. The value of the shares bought buy a number of the 'faithful supporters' had dramatically increased as land for housing was highly sought after.[2]

29th April 1953

Twenty members of the Trowbridge, Chippenham & District Employment Committee visited Westinghouse. This included their chairman Alderman Wilfred Ewart Vince, who was impressed with the work being carried out and thanked the company for their invitation. The distinguished visitors were welcomed by Michael James Hathaway, personnel superintendent, on behalf of Herbert Arthur Cruse CBE, director and general manager. They were then shown around all departments, explaining the various operations and how the company supplied brakes, signals and electrical equipment all over the world.[3]

30th April 1672

On this day, Benjamin Flower registered his home as a religious meeting house. It was recorded as either Independent or

1   *Salisbury & Winchester Journal*, 5 May 1860.
2   Twydell, pp.92-94
3   *Wiltshire Times*, 9 May 1953.

Presbyterian in denomination. Flower was described sarcastically as the 'Bishop of Chippenham' by the Corsham vicar in 1674. He was a nonconformist preacher and son of the vicar of Castle Combe.

Charles II hoped to encourage religious toleration with the Declaration of Indulgence of 1672. Dissenters were allowed to worship in specially licensed meeting places, and Flower was one of the first to do so. Parliament did not support the declaration however, and the persecution continued.[1]

MAY

1st May 1932

A 'phenomenal thunderstorm', accompanied by severe flooding, caused the town to be divided in two. It was probably the worst May flood for centuries.

Flooding of Bath Road, 1932. Chippenham Museum collection

The thunder was described as 'ear-splitting cracks…like the explosion of a monster cannon' and lasted for four hours that afternoon. This came with 'an accompaniment of a more vivid display

1   *Civic Society Bulletin*, issue 99, Spring 2001.

of celestial fireworks than many have ever previously seen'. The flood water reached 18-feet above the normal level. At the Nestlés factory, the height was only a few inches below that of 1926, but at the bridge it was a couple of inches above. Traffic became stuck either side and many people gave up getting home that evening and stayed with friends or relatives.

As the water receded, it left behind a large number of freshwater mussels, along with tons of sand which was saved for making cement.

The mail which was collected that day in the upper part of the town, needed to be taken to Stanley Halt on the Calne Branch line by road, then by train to the Sorting Office. This was a diversion of 6 miles instead of a journey of just quarter of a mile. Boats were considered for this task, but deemed unsafe due to whirlpools and the speed of the water. One whirlpool inside Pond's Island Store whisked empty bottle cases around inside, ripping off the doors.[1]

Severe weather events like this were the reason why improvements to the river were deemed necessary in the 1960s.

2nd May 1554

A Town Charter was granted by Queen Mary during the first year of her reign. It proclaimed that Chippenham 'shall be a free Borough Corporate in deed, fact and name for ever, of one bailiff and twelve burgesses'. Two of these burgesses were to attend Parliament. Plans to maintain the town bridge and the causeway were set out within the document. Funds were to be raised through the rent from lands given to the borough.

Henry Farnewell (alias Goldney) was already bailiff at the time and was nominated to carry on this role and to be the first named on the new charter. The bailiff position was then chosen annually on Michaelmas Day. Meetings of the bailiff and burgesses were held in the upper room of the Yelde Hall, whilst the freemen and under-bailiff met in the hall itself downstairs.[2]

The charter also gave permission for markets to be held at set dates each year.

1   *Wiltshire Times*, 7 May 1932.
2   Platts, pp.9-12.

The older parts of Chippenham Community Hospital were built in the 1850s for use as the Union Workhouse.

3rd May 1909

Fifty-two 'tramps' in the Chippenham Casual Ward 'mutinied' by refusing to carry out stone breaking as ordered. Using the tools they were supplied with for the job, they became violent. A porter was hit and a door damaged. Escalation of the situation was averted due to diplomacy of the workhouse master.[1]

Casual wards offered food and shelter for the night in return for work the next morning. Vagrants would then have to move on, as the workhouse was exclusively for inmates from the parish.

4th May 1940

Depression caused by ill health led to the tragic death of Albert Edward Adams, former Borough Surveyor for Chippenham Town Council. He was found dead from coal gas poisoning at his home in Bristol Road. Adams was 69 years old and had retired in April 1936 after

1   *Evening Express*, 3 May 1909.

40 years in his post. He was responsible for many important housing schemes and for designing the layout of John Coles Park.

During the First World War he carried out an honorary position for the Government at Westinghouse, for which he received a personal letter of thanks from then Prime Minister Lloyd George.

He had a large circle of friends made through his various club memberships. He was a member of the sports club, golf club and Chippenham Park Bowls Club. He also attended the Chippenham Literary & Scientific Institute.

Adams was found lying by his gas fire in his bedroom, his head on a pillow and the gas tap switched on. He had been suffering since having a stroke a few years earlier. Although not severely reducing his mobility, his participation in sports that he loved so much, was affected and this coupled with unfounded worries about money and the war, led him to take his own life.[1]

5th May 1911

Sir Audley & Lady Neeld declared the new cattle market open. Mayor Small, Alderman John Coles, Alderman Edmund Mainley Awdry, Colonel Sir George Helme, Mr & Mrs Rooke of The Ivy and Albert John Townsend were amongst those present. *God Save the King* was sung.[2] The new market covered the sites of the old cheese market and the George Hotel Yard. Messrs Downing & Rudman carried out the building work under the direction of architect Thomas Holt Fogg. There was accommodation for 400 cattle, 300 sheep and 120 pigs.

Market Hall (now known as the Neeld Hall) was built, joining the cattle market to the town hall. 80 ft long and 40 ft wide with 'roof trusses designed with curved steel ribs and tie-bar kept well up', to encourage the flow of sound around the building, made by Messrs Phipps & Son of Old Road. Seating accommodation was provided for 600 because as well as market purposes, the hall was designed with concerts and performances in mind.[3] The Neeld Hall was refurbished most recently in 2015, providing comfortable seating for 217 people.

1   *Wiltshire Times*, 11 May 1940.
2   *Wiltshire Times*, 13 May 1911.
3   *Wiltshire Times*, 6 May 1911.

6th May 2000

The town was gripped by football fever on this day as Chippenham Town FC played in the FA Vase final against Deal Town. Although Chippenham lost 1-0, it was still a proud moment in the club's history, with 13,000 supporters travelling to London. This was also one of the last matches to be played under the twin towers of the old Wembley Stadium.

Chippenham Town Football Club supporters at Wembley. Photograph - Julie Davies.

Chippenham Livestock Market, 27 June 1980. Photograph - Bakers of Nailsea, Butchers.

7th May 1951

Forty years after the opening of the cattle market in town, a new home was opened at Cocklebury Road. Initially, it was only an 'attested' cattle section, as the first stage of a larger plan. The opening was officiated by Harold Woolley, former Deputy President of the National Farmers Union.

The council had bought the nine acres of land at Cocklebury adjoining the railway in 1939 for the purpose of moving the market, but there was a delay due to the war and the necessary subsequent Whitehall permission.[1]

8th May 1869

A man named William Fortune died at Swindon aged 68 and was buried at Derry Hill near Chippenham. In accordance with his last will and testament, his whole coffin was painted yellow, as a 'symbol of his Liberal political principles'.[2]

1   *Wiltshire Times,* 12 May 1951.
2   *Reynolds' Newspaper,* 30 May 1868

9th May 1982

The much loved, and much missed, Monkton Park open-air swimming pool, hosted BBC TVs *It's a Knockout!* This was the last in the series of the inter-town competition to decide who would represent Great Britain in the Belgian heat of European game show *Jeux san Frontières,* in Ghent.

There was a maritime theme that included paddle steamers, a shark chase and a 'marathon' run by giant sailors.

Chippenham was competing against Ross on Wye and Gloucester (who went on to win by one point). The Chippenham team members included Chris Ashe, Karen Colly, Dawn Freer, Hughie Irwin, Les Jeffries, David Oakley, Leigh Robertson and Sally Wright. Their mascot was a real life camel which children took turns to ride. It was shown on BBC1 on 30 July and comedian Tom O'Connor was the guest presenter.[1]

Souvenir programme from 'It's a Knockout.' Photograph - Sarah Teal.

There was approximately 3,000 spectators for which temporary stands were erected next to the swimming pool. The Carnival Queen and her attendants were also present.

Due to significant overspending on the event, North Wiltshire District Council were left with a bill of almost £10,000. This was not helped by the lower than anticipated ticket and programme sales.

10th May 1913

The new tennis courts and bowling green added to the Chippenham Cricket Field, were formally opened. These cost the sports club almost £100. Club President Robert Long led the proceedings in front of a large crowd and afterwards he and the mayor played a game of bowls, which was won by Mr Long.[2]

1   jsf.hiddentigerbooks.co.uk.
2   *Wiltshire Times*, 14 May 1938.

11th May 1968

Less than a month after his controversial 'Rivers of Blood' speech in Birmingham, Enoch Powell arrived in Chippenham.

At the Girls School, he spoke about trade unionism, saying that 'conspiracies were already afoot to convince the public that the trade unions were responsible, wholly or partly for rising prices and the falling value of money'.

Outside, a picket was set up by anti-racism student protesters from Bristol University. The police were ready with a plan to cope with any eventuality after receiving a student pamphlet calling for a demonstration. This was headed 'demonstrate against racialism, against Powell, against fascism, for a socialist alternative,' and called on workers and students to organise to 'drive racialists back into their holes.'

On route to the rally, Powell was mobbed by shouting demonstrators, who were mainly students, chanting 'Powell out!'. One young girl jumped in front of his car causing a sudden halt. It eventually took twenty policemen to clear safe passage for the minister. Powell drove his own car and arrived earlier than expected, then was met by Chippenham Conservative MP Daniel Awdry and over 600 local Conservatives, who came to listen to him talk.[1]

12th May 1937

The coronation of King George VI was celebrated in the streets. Church bells were rang and a service held in the market place which included singing and performances from the British Legion and Salvation Army bands.

Various sporting fixtures took place at John Coles Park. Dog racing was staged at Hardenhuish Park, open to all breeds 'except greyhounds and longdogs'. A cricket match took place in the afternoon between Chippenham Town 1st XI and Westinghouse 1st XI.

Schools had tea parties and children were given coronation souvenirs.

In the evening there was a military display, boxing, a carnival dance and a firework display.[2]

---

1 *Chippenham News*, 17 May 1968.
2 Souvenir Programme, Spinke, Chippenham.

Downing Street residents celebrate the Coronation of King George VI. Photograph - Paula Champion.

13th May 1954

Mr Upton, manager of Finlay's tobacconist shop in the high street, got up from his chair to serve a customer, when suddenly a large block of stone crashed down on where he was sat only seconds earlier. Other pieces of stone hit his desk and the floor, whilst glass landed on another chair in which a traveller had just been sitting. It was discovered that the stone was dislodged when lightning struck the top of the three-storey building during a thunderstorm just before 1pm. Mr Upton would have most certainly been killed if he had still been sitting.[1]

14th May 1941

It was the funeral of James Bakewell Warrilow of 36 Malmesbury Road, who died aged 81. As a boy, he started work at the offices of solicitors, Messrs Wood & Awdry. Later he began his gunsmith business in Factory Lane until the premises was demolished for a proposed market extension in 1910. From then on he ran his business from home at Albany House, New Road.

1   *Wiltshire Times*, 15 May 1954.

For many years, Warrilow was a member of the Royal Wiltshire Yeomanry and twice won the Major AW Neeld Challenge cup for best marksman. He was also a poll clerk at all Chippenham elections for 50 years. In hi spare time he was a cricket umpire and referee for Chippenham Ladies Hockey Club.

A widower who had two sons, both died whilst serving their country in the First World War and two daughters, one of whom was married to Captain William Russell who was a football referee.[1] Russell was the only referee from Swindon to ever officiate at an FA Cup final, the 1924 'Rainy Day' final at Wembley. Programmes for this match can fetch up to £6000, as few survived, because many were used as makeshift umbrellas on the day.

15th May 1944

Master Fruiterer & Greengrocer John Banks was killed, after his home at 74 Wood Lane was attacked by an enemy aircraft in the early hours of the morning. Banks was dressing when he was struck in the head by cannon fire. He died later that day at the cottage hospital on London Road.

John Banks is buried at London Road Cemetery close to his brother Bertie, the stable lad who died in the Little George fire in 1903.

The home of Mrs Kingston nearby was also hit but fortunately none of the occupants were hurt. At Mrs Archard's, another cannon shell pierced the roof, travelled through the house and eventually fell harmlessly on the mat in the hall downstairs.[2]

16th May 1975

The Brooke Bond Oxo factory closed without any warning to its 168 employees.[3] A company spokesman said that the closure was due to

---

1   *Wiltshire Times*, 17 May 1941.
2   chippenham1939-1945.weebly.com
3   Chamberlain, J.A., (1976), p.141.

An OXO Christmas Party. Photograph - Peter Jefferies.

the 'present economic situation'.[1] The UK was near the end of a recession which had been marked by strikes and the 'Three Day Week'.

The redundancies came despite rumours of an impending closure being quashed when reassurances were given by the the managing director earlier in the year.

The factory opened in November 1939 and was one of only two that made the famous Oxo cube at that time, with all exported Oxo cubes being made there. The site was formerly home to a mill owned by the West of England Cloth Company.[2] The opening in Chippenham was part of a planned evacuation of food production away from London at the start of the Second World War, to less vulnerable areas.

The name changed to Brooke Bond Oxo in 1968-1969 when the two companies amalgamated. It was extended in 1970 to establish a cannery for the new Fray Bentos tinned beef and chicken curry flavours, with a production rate of up to 50,000 cans a day.[3] The Chippenham factory was also responsible for the successful trial and introduction of onion flavoured oxo cubes.

1   *Reading Evening Post*, 22 May 1975.
2   *Somerset Standard*, 15 February 1974.
3   *Wiltshire Times*, 21 September 1970.

17th May 1983

Students of the technical college at Cocklebury Road were shocked to find a large deposit of tadpoles in the grounds, which appeared shortly after a thunderstorm. It is believed that a waterspout lifted them from the river and dropped them there.[1]

18th May 1948

Four members of the Chippenham Sea Cadets broke the Devizes to Westminster Canoe Race record. The 140 miles were covered almost six hours quicker than the previous time set. This was despite the adverse tides and headwinds encountered towards the end of the route. The two canoes used were named 'Princess Elizabeth' and 'Princess Margaret'.

Petty Officer Roy Parker of Beanacre, Leading Seamen David South of The Hamlet, Chippenham, Frank Attrill of Melksham and Geoffrey Busby also of Beanacre, were the participating cadets. When they returned to Chippenham they were presented to an audience at the Gaumont Cinema.[2]

The four Chippenham Sea Cadets (centre front row) who rowed from Devizes to Westminster in a record time in 1948. Photograph - Martin Sausins.

1   Meaden, G.T., (1984), "Shower of Tadpoles...," *Journal of Meteorology*.
2   *Wiltshire Times*, 22 May 1948.

19th May 1841

Two 'respectably attired' men went into the house of Mrs Ann Goldney of the Bear Inn and asked for a room. Whilst there, they were able to freely move around the house without causing suspicion. They discovered that Mrs Goldney's bedroom door was open so went inside and helped themselves to 18 silver spoons and a silver watch. They unsuccessfully tried to force open a drawer that had £300 in cash inside, before making a getaway. When the landlady discovered what had happened she immediately alerted Superintendent Wright. He organised search parties on all routes out of the town and soon the pair were found, two miles out on Bath Road, with all the valuables in their possession.[1]

20th May 1892

The last broad gauge train passed through Chippenham from Paddington then on to the west country. After this date, only standard gauge, or narrow gauge as it was known, would be used by the Great Western Railway.

21st May 1915

A large fire took hold at Waterford Mills in Factory Lane at around 1 am. The fire brigade under the command of Captain Buckle and Albert Edward Adams, Borough Surveyor, arrived to deal with the situation. Adams ensured a sufficient water supply and pressure could be secured at the waterworks nearby.

The factory, famous for its 'West of England' cloth, was split into two parts by the road. The fire started on the older 'right-hand side' nearest the river. The fire brigade stopped the fire from moving across the bridge and from spreading to the adjoining tannery. In the end, however, half of the factory was destroyed. The staff had been working on a large French Army order up until the previous day.[2] All 200 workers were made unemployed. These were mostly women and children as the majority of townsmen were serving in the war.

Waterford Mills was established in 1707, and was the only cloth factory in Chippenham to survive into the 20th century. It reopened

---

1 *Wiltshire Gazette*, 27 May 1841.
2 *North Wilts Herald*, 21 May 1915.

The Cloth Factory Fire of 1915. Chippenham Museum collection

after the fire but closed for good in 1930.[1] The surviving buildings were later used by Brooke Bond Oxo, Mattesons Meats then Hygrade.[2]

22nd May 1939

The Astoria cinema in Marshfield Road opened for the first time, showing 'The Citadel' starring Robert Donat. Built in the Art Deco style by architect William Henry Watkins, it was originally meant to be much larger with an addition of restaurant on the roof. The finished building had a capacity of just over 1,100 and benefitted from a spacious free car park nearby for over 200 cars. The inside colour scheme was rose, with silver curtains for the screens. A Western Electric Mirrophonic sound system was installed. Eric Harris was the first manager.[3]

In 1967, Star Cinemas Circuit of Leeds took over, changing the name to 'Studio Cinema' and it was divided to allow for a bingo hall on the lower floor. Then, in 1973, the remaining screen was divided so two films could run at the same time, with the new name 'Studios 1+2'.

The cinema was operated by Cannon from 1985 until 1994, when a purchase by Picturedrome Theatres reinstated the original 'Astoria' name.

1   *Wiltshire Times*, 27 September 1930
2   *Civic Society Bulletin*, Issue 69, April 1994.
3   *The Era*, 25 May 1939.

The Astoria with its modern facelift by Reel Cinemas. An asset to the town.

The Angel Bingo Club closed suddenly in August 2009, which could provide a space for three additional screens. The installation of these eventually began in May 2018 and was completed on 28th August 2018. The cinema is now part of Reel, who have secured its future with the impressive refurbishment. The Astoria name has been preserved.

23rd May 2012

The 2012 Olympic Flame was carried through the town, albeit half an hour late, having taken a wrong turn in the mist outside of Bristol. Further delay was caused by the crowds trying to get close to the torch in Chippenham.[1]

There were six torchbearers after the arrival on Bristol Road, who covered the route through the Market Place and the Causeway to London Road. These were; Robert Warwick, Samuel Way, William Cruickshank, Roger Crang, Phoebe Kemp and Tom Perkins.

---

1 *Guardian*, 23 May 2012.

CHIPPENHAM

St Andrew's Bellringers were on duty whilst the torch relay passed by. (L to R) Bob Mustow, Joanna Wheatland, Tony Mustow, Nick Watts, Jean Cary, Lin Drummond-Harris, Caroline Emerson, Rod Brown & Morley Bray. Photograph - Joanna Wheatland.

Phoebe Kemp carries the Olympic Flame through the Market Place and on to the Causeway.

24th May 1969

An 'Unidentified Flying Object' was observed over the high street. Shortly after 11pm, an 'orange coloured disc' emitting a pulsating light, was seen travelling over the town centre. It first emerged into view from the direction of River Street, crossed over the high street, then the river, before disappearing from view in the direction of Monkton Park.

It was moving at the speed of a small aircraft but made no noise. The sighting was witnessed by at least a dozen people who were standing in the high street including two police officers.[1]

25th May 1949

Chippenham United Supporters Club held a victory dinner at the Neeld Hall. It was the end of their first season as a professional club, yet they had already enjoyed considerable success as champions of Western League Division Two, and by reaching the FA Cup First Qualifying Round. Further success was enjoyed by the reserve side winning the Dr Elliot Cup and the youth side were joint holders of the Chippenham & District Youth League title. The supporters club, with its 1400 members, was recognised as crucial to the success they had enjoyed. All three trophies were on display at the dinner. Guests included Louis Page, who was manger of Swindon Town and Ted Davis, an Arsenal scout and former manager of Bath City.[2]

This menu from United's Victory Dinner includes signatures of the players.

26th May 1972

The first Folk Festival was held in Lacock on Spring Bank Holiday weekend. A medieval street fayre in the village the year before, inspired Nigel Bonallack to start the festival in 1972. Tom Geddes remembers that it was a 'fabulous weekend, but unseasonably cold and windy. Not ideal camping weather!'

1   *Flying Saucer Review*, Sept/Oct 1969, Vol.15, No.5, p.19.
2   Twydell, pp.70-71.

CHIPPENHAM

From 1974, the event was split between the National Trust village and Chippenham, where it had moved to completely by 1984.

27th May 1951

Sixty years of Chippenham Cricket Club was celebrated with an anniversary match at Hardenhuish Park. The opponents were a Wiltshire

A programme from the Lacock Folk Festival, 1972. Poster - Tom Geddes.

county side captained by Sir William Becher and included future England football player John Atyeo, who went on to sign his first professional contract with Bristol City Football Club, less than three weeks later.

In the earlier days of the club, matches were played at the Ivy Fields, where visitors included world-famous cricketer WG Grace.[1]

John Atyeo went on to play for England even though he was at Second Division football club Bristol City.

28th May 1960

Monkton Park swimming pool officially opened on this hot day!

---

1   *Wiltshire Times*, 19 May 1951.

Residents were invited to use it free of charge on this occasion. Mayor Reginald George Archard declared the pool open from 4.30pm. Clubs from Swindon and Bristol showed their skills with swimming and diving displays.

The pool was built by G Percy Trentham Ltd for £51,296.[1]

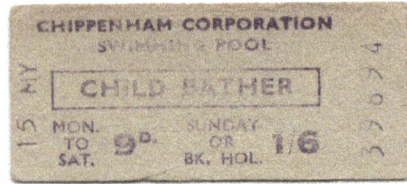

A child ticket to swim at Chippenham's outdoor pool.

Mayor Reginald George Archard with Mayoress Eileen Archard. Photograph - David Letten (Grandson).

29th May 1964

It was a Friday and the town was busy as the market was being held. Unfortunately, poor planning meant that a haulier, with police assistance, had decided to use this day to move an abnormal load through Chippenham.

A prefabricated cylinder over 120 feet in length negotiated the town's roads causing 'widespread congestion and inconvenience'.

Chippenham MP Daniel Awdry raised the issue in parliament to the Minister for Transport. It was questioned whether railway line closures and a lack of movement on completing the M4 were to blame. The Minister pointed out that deciding the route of the motorway had not been easy, and claimed that construction would have begun much sooner if 'the people in Wiltshire had been a little more accommodating'.[2]

This turned out to be the first of four similar loads which passed through the town over four consecutive Mondays.

1 *Wiltshire Times*, 19 January 1990.
2 *Hansard*, Commons Sitting, 1 July 1964.

30th May 1841

The Great Western Railway, designed and built by Brunel, reached the town, when the Hay Lane terminus to Chippenham section was opened on 31 May 1841. The first train to arrive here, however, was the day before, when a trial trip took place that caused 'no small amount of excitement' amongst the locals.

The men working on the line were offered large sums of money to encourage them to finish on time, which they did so by working around the clock. They were able to lay down the final rails just before the test train arrived with the 'last screw being driven in a few minutes before it made its appearance'.[1]

A man named William Ferris passed on his memories of this event to notable diarist Francis Kilvert. He described how it was a hot day and he was 'foddering' near the line when he heard a 'roaring in the air'. He expected a storm to roll in from the direction of Christian Malford but the weather was fine. The roaring sound came closer, then he saw the train shoot by, dust flying as it passed.[2]

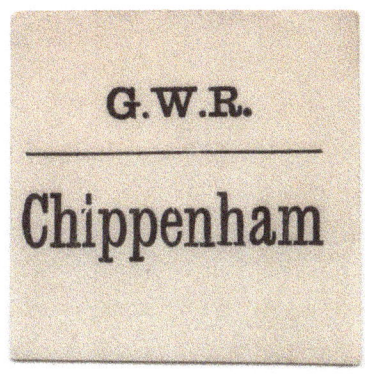

A Great Western Railway luggage label with Chippenham as the destination.

31st May 1924

An event described as the worst storm for many years, occurred over the district. Meteorologists believed that two storms were responsible for the deluge which ensued late in the afternoon that day.

In Lacock, basements filled with rainwater and at Manor Farm, James Newman lost a cow to a lightning strike.

In Burton, the water ran through houses and in Christian Malford and the hamlet of Avon, roads were impassable.[3] Fields all around Chippenham were flooded.

At Cherry Patch in Biddestone, a cottage was struck by lightning. The bolt made a hole in the chimney pot, shot into a bedroom below

---

1 *Devizes and Wiltshire Gazette*, 3 June 1841.
2 *Kilvert's Diary*.
3 *North Wiltshire Herald*, 6 June 1924.

smashing all glass items and left a scorch mark on the door. It carried on below into the kitchen, where Mr and Mrs Edwards were hit by falling masonry, and their child, just taken from a bath, was flung from Mrs Edwards' arms. Mrs Edwards also received a burn to the foot when the floor was hit by the electricity. The family were extremely lucky not to receive more serious injuries.[1]

JUNE

1st June 1896

Lowden School opened on this day, it's necessity due to the housing expansion on the western side of town. It was situated on the corner of Woodlands Road and Sheldon Road, now occupied by Marlborough

Lowden School, c1922. Photograph - Trisha Lewis. Teresa's mother is second from the left, third row from the front, with the fringe she had cut herself going from ear to ear. Another girl in the centre of the second row from the front, with shoulder length hair and light dress, was later Mrs Smith, a midwife at Greenways.

Court. The land was purchased by the vicar and churchwardens in 1895, for £110 from John Smith. Built by Messrs Light & Smith, a fair distance

1 *Wiltshire Times*, 7 June 1924.

was kept between the frontage onto Sheldon Road, with the view to building a teacher's house at a later date.

The opening ceremony was conducted by Archdeacon Robeson. Initially, there were 70 pupils on the roll, yet only two weeks later an infant department opened for a further 69. The first headmaster was George Dear and he stayed in the position until retirement on 31 December 1932.[1]

2nd June 1953

The coronation of Queen Elizabeth II was celebrated. Church bells rang out and a combined religious service was held in Market Place.

Most people in the town were able to watch the coronation and procession on a television set, either using their own, with neighbours or at one set up by the Coronation Committee in a public building.

From 3pm there was a programme of events to entertain, including an unusual game of football using a rugby ball between a team from both Chippenham Town and United against the rugby club. The Army Cadets, Sea Cadets and Fire Brigade all put on demonstrations. A spectacular firework display and the Chippenham Town Silver Band were other highlights. Clifford Ronald Phillips, the borough surveyor, supervised the erection of 160 columns on either side of the road between Market Place and Western Arches. These had shields, flags and bunting and were linked with streamers.

The day before, two trees were planted at St Andrew's Hospital by the Mayor George Lane Culverwell.

Coronation mugs and a crown piece, were presented to the parents of all babies born in the town on the day and to those celebrating their Diamond or Golden Wedding anniversary.

Residential streets were decorated with some households working together to produce fantastic results, Downing Street being a notable example.[2]

3rd June 1895

A short-lived Salvation Army barracks was opened. It was built at the 'rear of Mr Burgess's premises' near the town bridge, almost entirely

1   Chamberlain, J.A., (1976), p.98.
2   *Wiltshire Times*, 6 June 1953.

by the soldiers of the local Salvation Army corps. The roof and walls were made of corrugated iron, lined with matchboard. There was a capacity for 300 seated persons. This structure was replaced by the Citadel only eight years later.

4th June 1940

An extension was opened at St Margaret's Convent School, Rowden Hill. This was built using funds set aside to accommodate evacuees in the town, who were moving out from the big cities because of the risk of the bombing raids, during the Second World War. The extension is still in use today at the centre of the St Mary's School site.

5th June 1954

From 1–5 June, an exhibition to celebrate 400 years of Chippenham's history, was held in the town hall. Visitors were able to view historical items including the 1554 town charter, old maps, photographs and other objects relating to the town's past.[1]

Silver Jubilee street party at Downing Street. Photograph - Tim Gatherum.

1   Wilson, A. & M., (1991), p.131.

6th June 1929

The day after the Epsom Derby, James Frederick Barnard was fined £5 for street-betting. In his defence, Barnard argued that there must have been £10,000,000 in bets passed on the day and it was 'very hard a man cannot have a bit...without being 'copped' by the police'.[1] The race was won by 'Trigo' at 33/1. Whether Barnard backed the right horse or not, we'll never know!

7th June 1977

Street parties were held to mark the Queen's Silver Jubilee. One of the most notable was at Downing Street. The arrangements there were made by Heather Hulbert, Joan Baker, Cora Townsend, Evelyn Kilmartin, Joan Radcliffe, CW McClusky, Judith Burge and Maureen Davies. Fifty children received commemorative mugs. The street was shut from 2pm and 6pm. A room at the Railway Inn was on standby incase rain threatened the event.[2]

8th June 1971

The foundation stone was laid at the new masonic hall in Emery Lane.

The first Masonic hall in Chippenham was built in 1933 behind the high street, on a piece of land that is now covered by part of the Emery Gate shopping precinct. Brother William Millman Brown Burridge, the junior ward, had offered the new site as a gift. The total cost of the build was thought to be £1870, including the furniture.

Later, a 'very advantageous price' was offered for the old site, so the new masonic hall could be built

William Burridge, who gifted land off the High Street for the Masons. Photograph - Nick Burridge.

1   *Guardian*, 7 June 1929.
2   *Wiltshire Times*, 20 May 1972.

in Emery Lane. The foundation stone from the earlier building, having been moved, was re-laid at the new hall.[1]

9th June 1814

The celebrations for Napoleon's abdication and ratification of the Treaty of Paris, reached their height with a dinner held at the White Hart (now Iceland), at a cost of 3s per guest. The next day the town was illuminated.[2] The festivities had started on the previous Tuesday when an estimated 1800 poor of the town were 'regaled with roast beef and plum pudding'.[3]

10th June 1804

The Old Baptist Chapel in Gutter Lane (now Chapel Lane) was opened by Paul Porter of Bath. There were around 100 people in attendance. Porter was previously the pastor of Somerset Street Chapel in Bath.

Before a font was installed in 1818, baptisms took place in the river at Westmead. This was especially unpopular in winter!

The chapel itself is a stone building which was completely square in shape when built, but was extended in Victorian times, and can now comfortably hold two hundred worshippers.

Inside Old Baptist Chapel just off the High Street at the Heritage Open Day in 2018.

1   pglwilts.org.uk/lodges/north-wiltshire/lansdowne-lodge-of-unity
2   Chamberlain, J.A., (1976), p.21.
3   *Salisbury & Winchester Journal*, 20 June 1814.

The first attendees originated from the Independent Chapel, later Tabernacle United Reformed Church, in Emery Lane. Deep internal divisions among the membership at the Tabernacle in 1804, principally due to the ordinance of 'Believers Baptism', led to the break away church forming.

11th June 1831

A council meeting was held to consider the 'distressed state of the lower class of people of Ireland'. It was agreed that it was a Christian duty to help such people and a subscription should be opened. The religious ministers of the town were asked to make collections in their respective places of worship. It was also recognised that legislative pressure should be used to seek change for those in poverty in Ireland. Plans were made to draw up a petition for presentation to Parliament. A committee, with Mr Poole as treasurer, was created to collate the funds and petitions. A book was left in the bank for subscriptions to be entered and a copy of all these resolutions was sent to the Bath & Cheltenham Gazette.[1]

12th June 1926

Prime Minister Stanley Baldwin addressed a mass Conservative demonstration at Hardenhuish Park. The plan was for him to speak from a specially built platform in the open air, but the inclement weather had turned the park into a swamp, so a large marquee was hastily erected. A civic reception was also cancelled due to a 'recent indisposition' of Mr Baldwin's (he had caught a 'severe chill' whilst travelling from London to Edinburgh the week before).

He and Mrs Baldwin had arrived directly from their Chequers residence and received a warm welcome as the car passed through the town. There were an estimated 15,000 people at the event which was held in connection with a Unionist fete.[2]

The visit came a month after the 1926 General strike, which was called by the Trades Union Congress (TUC), who failed to force the British government to act to prevent wage reductions and worsening conditions for 1.2 million locked-out coal miners

1   Goldney, p.153.
2   *The Times*, 14 June 1926

13th June 1894

At 7.30 am a fast goods train was passing at a point near the top of Lowden Hill, when one of the trucks in the middle of the train came off the tracks. It travelled a further quarter of a mile before the driver and guard could stop it safely. The line was blocked and a breakdown gang from Swindon were needed to assist Inspector Baldwin and the 'permanent way' staff to get the truck back on the rails. Impressively, this was done and dusted by 11 am. The gradual stopping of the train by the skilful driver prevented what could have been a very serious accident from taking place.[1]

14th June 2008

Fuel tanker driver strikes led to panic buying at petrol stations in Chippenham. Soon, all the supermarket pumps were dry as well as the Esso garage at Cepen Park. Only the two Total garages at Rowden and London Road still had a supply, and long queues soon formed at these.[2]

The strike, by hundreds of Shell tanker drivers, was over pay. Panic buying nationally, caused a 25% rise in fuel purchases, which led to closure of petrol stations when they began to run dry. The South West was one of the worst affected areas.

The original tablet from the stone marker at the Chippenham end of Maud Heath's Causeway, on display in Chippenham Museum.

15th June 1974

It was the Quincentenary of Maud Heath's Causeway. 500th Anniversary celebrations took place. It was a day of pageantry; a Christian service at the top of Wick Hill was followed by a procession to Monkton Park by adults and school children in period costumes. Various folk dancers and musicians performed throughout the day and a barn dance was held in the Neeld Hall in the evening.

1   *Bristol Mercury*, 14 June 1894.
2   *Gazette & Herald*, 14 June 2008.

Museum Curator Mr Chamberlain compiled a short souvenir book on the history of the causeway and gave a public lecture. Four new benches were added along the route and a commemorative sundial was erected at East Tytherton.

16th June 1881

William Gregory died after being gored by a bull at James Long's Rowden Farm.[1] On the night of the 1881 census, William was listed as living in a cottage opposite the New Inn (now The Pheasant) with his wife Elizabeth and son Solomon. His occupation was recorded as 'Cowman'.

17th June 1933

The annual Cottage Hospital Carnival was held, but this was the first in which a carnival queen was chosen. She was crowned on the evening of 15th June at the Neeld Hall with her four maids of honour invested at the same time. Vera Townsend, the daughter of Mayor and Mayoress Townsend was chosen as queen, along with her four maids, as the 'prettiest five' by a 'committee of Bristol experts'.[2]

The maids of honour were; Miss Hilda Roberts of Ladyfield Road, Miss Audrey Wheeler of Wood Lane, Miss Kathleen Gibbons of Colerne and Miss Rose Sprules of Biddestone.[3]

The carnival was opened by

The Singing Fools' performed at the 1930 Chippenham Hospital Carnival. Photograph - Chris Dunster.

1   *Wiltshire Times*, 18 June 1881.
2   *Wiltshire Times*, 29 April 1933.
3   *Western Daily Press*, 19 June 1933.

Sir Audley Neeld and continued throughout a spell of heavy rain.

The Mayor acknowledged that for his daughter to be crowned queen, that there must have been 'something of a wangle' but he made it clear that this was not the case. Not only did he have no idea of his daughter's entry until he saw her picture in the paper, but initially he wasn't very happy that she had even entered. He was ultimately pleased and proud of her achievement.

Miss Philomena Thornton and Miss Joan Holder of Chippenham Secondary School were pages, one responsible for the queen's robe, the other her crown and sceptre.[1]

Messrs Jennings Amusement fair was in attendance, 'The Great Risko' performed a balancing act up on top of an 80-foot ladder and the new British Legion band, under Bandmaster Frank Fields, played at the front of the carnival procession.

18th June 1880

William Watson of Monkton Hill, railway labourer for the GWR, had kept a nest of young linnets in a cage, by a hedge at the goods station. He had fed them the previous evening, but the next morning when he returned the birds were missing and instead a snake was in the cage. It transpired that the snake, which was three-foot-long, had squeezed inside the cage, but after swallowing the birds whole, couldn't get back out again![2]

During the late Victorian and Edwardian periods, it was common to keep linnets because of their melodic song. There are numerous cultural references to the linnet. Perhaps the best known being in the 1919 music hall song 'Don't Dilly Dally on the Way (The Cock Linnet Song)'.

19th June 1883

An inquest was held due to the death of Mary Ann Salter, a 'servant girl' who had been in service for several years in London and had returned home pregnant. Her parents were Joseph and Ann Salter of The Butts.

Harriet Wigmore, a herbalist, living in nearby Calne, was judged to have performed an abortion.[3] The inquest returned a verdict of murder

---

1 *Wiltshire Times*, 17 June 1933
2 *Swindon Advertiser*, 26 June 1880.
3 Clarification through detailed research by Lucy Whitfield

and the coroner committed Wigmore for trial.[1]

It is not clear through the various reports, whether Harriet had actually intended to help Mary abort her baby. She was found guilty of manslaughter not murder, and was sentenced to ten years penal servitude.

On the 1881 census, Mary was listed as a cook for John Maitland, a chemist of Paddington, London. She was 33 when she died on 16 June and was buried at London Road Cemetery on 21 June.

Harriet could later be found in Roundway Asylum, Devizes on the 1901 census, listed as a 'Herbalist - Lunatic'.

Placards used during the Black Lives Matter protest. Chippenham Museum Collection.

20th June 2020

A Black Lives Matter protest was held at the Buttercross in Market Place. The event was attended by c200 protesters many carrying placards. Others stood guard at the war memorial because they were concerned that it may have been attacked, as seen at similar protests. These men made it clear that they were not against the BLM protest

1   *Birmingham Daily Post,* 20 June 1883.

but were concerned that some other groups may use the opportunity to cause trouble. A small police presence stood by but fortunately, it was not called into action. At one point the protestors 'took the knee' during a symbolic 8 minutes and 45-second silence. This was the same amount of time that George Floyd had a policeman's knee on his neck in the arrest that sparked the BLM protests worldwide.[1]

21st June 1955

An incident involving a boy found drunk on Station Hill was described as a 'deplorable case' by Inspector Reginald Frank Cuss at Chippenham Juvenile Court. On 8 April, a Good Friday, PC Townsend attended the scene after receiving a complaint from a resident. The boy was found lying on the pavement, completely incapable, with no memory after leaving the pub to his arrival at the police station. He did remember being bought 'rough cider' by a man, as he had no money of his own. After he was fined 10s, he said he had learned his lesson and would not drink again.[2]

22nd June 1887

Chippenham's celebration of Queen Victoria's Golden Jubilee fell on a Wednesday, the day after celebrations in London. The church bells began ringing at 8 am and at intervals throughout the day. Children were given medals to mark the occasion and after a church service, were led to 'the field' at Lowden by a fife and drum band, where they were entertained and took part in 'military sports'. After the children's tea, a public meat tea and fireworks display rounded off the day.

As part of the commemorations, Sir John Neeld gave over land in the Market Place for

One of the medals given to the schoolchildren of the town as a token of remembrance for the Queen's Jubilee of 1887

1 *Gazette & Herald,* 20 June 2020.
2 *Wiltshire Times,* 25 June 1955.

The Jubilee Institute, Market Place.

the erection of the Jubilee Institute. The cost of the building was later raised by public subscription.[1]

23rd June 1839

A chilver (female lamb) was stolen by a gang of 'desperadoes' who had been loitering in the town for some time and causing distress to many. The lamb belonged to Joseph Lewis and was kept in a field at Pewsham. Horrifically, the thieves slaughtered the animal on the spot, leaving its head and skin behind! In the hope of catching those responsible, a joint reward of £20 was put forward by Lewis and the Chippenham Prosecution Society.[2]

24th June 1837

A proclamation of Queen Victoria's Accession was read out in the Market Place.[3] She became Queen when her uncle William IV died on 20 June. Her Coronation took place a year later on 28 June 1838.

25th June 1899

Two notable incidents took place in the evening on this day. Mrs Hunt of London Road fell and broke her leg whilst going down some steps. Meanwhile, William Keene was sitting on a wall at the foot of Lowden Hill and was taken ill. When help came it became apparent it was serious, and he died before anything could be done. Heart disease was suspected as the cause.[4]

---

1 Platts, p 23
2 *Wiltshire Independent*, 4 July 1839.
3 Goldney, p.162.
4 *Bristol Mercury*, 27 June 1899.

Commemorative pin badge for Westinghouse Bowls Club's Golden Jubilee. Like many large employers, Westinghouse were conscious of encouraging their workforce to be fit and social.

26th June 1937

It was the grand opening of the Westinghouse Sports facilities. A new pavilion, hard tennis courts and a bowling green were declared open by one of England's most famous sports personalities of the time, Lord Burghley.

Burghley had won a gold medal at the 1928 Olympics in Amsterdam. He was the inspiration for the character of Lord Andrew Lindsay, played by Nigel Havers in the 1981 film *Chariots of Fire*.

The river Avon at 'Black Bridge' is deceptively calm on the surface.

27th June 1941

George Francis Billett of Rowden Road was bathing by the Black Bridge when he got into difficulty and had to be rescued by fellow bathers. He was unconscious when pulled out by his friends; Kenneth Smith of Railway House, Henry Page of Ladyfield Road and Reginald Cole of The Hamlet, who were able to successfully revive him at the riverbank. Meanwhile, Brian Timbrell of Lowden summoned the police. They probably saved Billett's life and he only needed a short spell in Chippenham Hospital.[1]

28th June 1989

Simulation of various emergencies including drowning, a road traffic collision and people collapsing, took place in the town as part of a training exercise. Thirty students from the Ambulance Training Centre

1   *Wiltshire Times*, 28 June 1941.

at Malmesbury Road volunteered to take part. All the sirens and rushing about caused great excitement in the town, as most of the population didn't know it wasn't real.[1]

29th June 2013

Popular Ironmongers Dentons closed its doors for the last time. The Park Lane business had many successful years, but eventually became a victim of rising overheads, falling sales and the loss of parking.[2]

Dentons Hardware. Photograph - Adrian Full.

After the death of previous owner Ken Terry, Dentons was taken on by Paul and Cilla Thatcher in 1999, adding to their other business at 2A Electrical. There had been a shop on the site since 1933, originally selling furniture, with Dentons itself in residence for 60 years.[3]

The building was in a poor state so was demolished and replaced with flats.

The Dentons name came from Arthur Benjamin Denton who died in 1968 age 72. Originally from Lancashire, he came to Chippenham in 1956 and bought the Ironmongers business in Park Lane. He retired in 1963 and lived at Derry Hill.[4]

1 *Gazette & Herald*, 29 June 1989.
2 www.diyweek.net, 1 July 2013.
3 *Civic Society Bulletin*, Issue 149, p.10.
4 Clipping from 1968, Garlick Collection.

This bonfire was erected for Queen Victoria's Diamond Jubilee on 22 June 1897. Chippenham Museum collection

30th June 1902

An 'immense' bonfire was lit on 'high ground at Englands' to celebrate the improved health of the King. The town crier proclaimed the event and at 10pm the mayor set light to the 30 foot stack of fagots, tar barrels and trees. A band played 'God save the King'.[1]

The King's coronation was originally set for 26 June but on the 24th he was diagnosed with appendicitis. This celebration was for the news that he was to make a full recovery. The coronation was rebooked and successfully held on 9 August 1902.

1   *Wiltshire County Advertiser*, 5 July 1902.

JULY

1st July 1937

The Sir Audley Arms public house opened on Audley Road. It was built by Messrs F Rendall and Sons Ltd of Devizes, for Ushers Brewery of Trowbridge, and stands on part of the Wiltshire Brick and Tile Company's former brickyard. They had made the bricks for building the pub in their adjoining yard, with 'Monks Park' stone for the dressings.

At the opening ceremony, Thomas Charles Usher, chairman of the brewery, handed a gilt key to Mayor George Lane Culverwell and a luncheon was held in the skittle alley. Sir Audley Neeld himself was unable to attend due to another important engagement, but he had already 'taken a keen interest' in the new pub.[1]

The Sir Audley Arms public house, Audley Road. Opened in 1937.

2nd July 1861

West Stuart Awdry, sisters Alicia and Amy Lowder, along with younger members of the Awdry family, were all boating on the river near Monkton House. Sometime between 7pm and 8pm, their two

---

1   *Wiltshire Times*, 3 July 1937.

boats collided on approaching the dead water area above the town mill. The smaller boat carrying the Lowder Sisters and West capsized. Alicia clung tightly to him and they both sank together. The Reverend Clarke was passing and rescued the other sister, who by strange coincidence lost her father in India by drowning. It was gone 11pm before the two bodies were recovered.[1]

Alicia Eirene Lowder, was buried 6 July, at Derry Hill. She was 16 years old. West Stuart Awdry was buried at Grittleton, also on 6 July, and was 20 years old.

3rd July 1618

Richard Berrye, a householder within the Borough of Chippenham, was 'found to be a common drunkard and person of evil behaviour', so was stripped of his rights and benefits of the borough lands.[2]

4th July 1953

Anthony 'Tony' Wedgwood Benn MP, spoke at a Labour Party Fete held at The Firs. The home of Chippenham United Football Club hosted a 'comprehensive programme' which included stalls, sideshows, children's sports and a fancy dress parade. Mrs Garrett put on a puppet show and arranged a demonstration of square dancing. A firework display closed the event.

Mr Benn spoke about the Cold War, the truce in Korea and how the UK should be able to think independently of America in terms of its own foreign policy. He also talked about how full employment in the UK and America was planned on a level of defence expenditure, so any end to the Cold War could cause an economic depression.

5th July 1920

On this day, a foundation stone was laid to mark the first phase of the Ladyfield housing estate. The inscription on the stone read;

> Corporation of Chippenham Borough Housing Scheme
> This stone was laid by the Mayor, Councillor Hyatt, July 5 1920

---

1   *Bath Chronicle* & Weekly Gazette, 4 July 1861.
2   Goldney, pp.46-47.

Houses in Palmer Street during construction. Postcard - Paula Champion

In line with the Housing and Town Planning Act 1919, which stated that all local authorities would be the duty bound to provide houses for the working classes, these 'workmen's dwellings' were built by Rudman's, on behalf of the council.

Three newly minted threepenny pieces, six pennies and one halfpenny with 1920 dates, were placed under the stone by the mayor, who declared the stone 'to be well and truly laid, and as the erection of dwellings is helpful to man, also to that end, to the glory of God'. He was presented with a silver trowel inscribed;

> Presented to the Mayor of Chippenham on the occasion of laying the foundation stone of the Borough housing scheme, 1920.

This trowel is now on display in Chippenham Museum.

The date of the ceremony was delayed to coincide with the launch of housing bonds that had been floated locally.

Lowden School took time out of lessons to attend with Headmaster George Dear. Miss Eva Hatherill presented a bouquet to the mayoress, who attended with Mayor Alderman Marshall, the Chairman of the Housing Committee, and Councillor Edward Newall Tuck, Vice Chairman of the Housing Committee, among others. Mr Marshall commented on how the cost of 12 cottages built in Wood Lane in 1914 would build three of the houses on this development. Mr Tuck made it clear that the new homes would go to who they were built for; those who fought for their country and the widows of those who didn't return.[1]

6th July 2000

A river of sewage flooded into shops on the high street causing extensive damage. A 'cloudburst' of torrential rain dumped a huge amount of water, overwhelming the sewers, lifting drain covers and pushing sewage out onto the street. The worst-hit shops were Superdrug, WHSmith and Roseby's, which were all six inches deep in water. The road was closed that evening by the fire brigade. Wessex Water, who disinfected the road, described what happened as a 'one in every ten years' event.

Managers from the three affected shops all agreed that they were fed up with having to suffer the consequences of inadequate drainage.[2]

7th July 1369

The Chippenham coat of arms are first recorded in a chantry lease, used by John Gode and John Enforde, to seal the lease of a house in the high street, then known as King's Street, on this date. The seal showed these arms suspended from a palm tree and represented manorial civic authority, as the manors of Sheldon and Rowden are shown. This design was adopted as the common seal of the borough in the 16th century, though there is speculation as to whether this was a revival or new tradition.

The coat of arms of Chippenham. This image is taken from a piece of WH Goss souvenir pottery.

8th July 1959

1   *Wiltshire Times*, 10 July 1920.
2   *Gazette & Herald*, 17 July 2000.

It was the official opening of the new secondary modern school for boys, later named Sheldon School. Those present included; Mr John Henry Bradley (Chief Education Officer for Wiltshire), Reverend Philip Snow (Vicar of Chippenham), Eric William Minter (Headmaster), Geoffrey Lloyd (Minister for Education), Joan Stopford Beale (Chair of Governors) and Alderman William Ewart Stevens (Chairman of the Wiltshire Education Committee).[1]

The Minister for Education heralded the opening of the comprehensive school, as part of a 'massive increase in educational opportunity at all levels', but made it clear he felt that grammar schools should be preserved.[2]

Eric Minter retired in 1966 and was awarded the OBE. The next headmaster, George Morgan, was appointed in 1967. Morgan managed the transition to a mixed comprehensive system and was the one who chose the name 'Sheldon' when the three schools became two comprehensives in 1975. Originally, Sheldon's catchment area was the south and east sides of the town, with Hardenhuish covering the north and west.[3]

9th July 1643

Hopton's Army were defeated at Lansdown on 8 July and retreated. The Royalists left Marshfield heading towards Chippenham en route to Oxford avoiding Malmesbury (now a parliamentary stronghold), through Wraxall and Giddeahall (A420). Just outside Chippenham they heard news that the Calvary of Waller (Roundheads) were on their tail. The Cornish regiment halted and offered Waller a fight on the 'level land between Biddestone in Chippenham but Waller declined. Both sides camped that night within talking distance of one another in the fields west of Chippenham'. This was the first real taste of the war for the town, for in the early hours of the 9th, detachments of the parliamentary calvary raced through Chippenham. There were dog fights between cavalry and infantry of both sides. A 'ferocious' cavalry charge took place near the northern edge of Pewsham Forest and afterwards a withdrawal

---

1 Chippenham *Civic Society Bulletin*, Sheldon School Celebrates Half Century, article by Caroline Fowke.
2 *Guardian*, 9 July 1959.
3 Chippenham *Civic Society Bulletin*, Sheldon School Celebrates Half Century, article by Caroline Fowke.

Civil War re-enactment on Island Park, July 2022.

was made southward towards Bromham.

10th July 1871

George Tompkins, the town surveyor, summoned Charles Butler, John Gainey and George Lair for causing deliberate damage to Arthur's Well. An employee of Mr Tompkins, John Knott, witnessed the three running away from the scene and on closer inspection saw that the well had been deliberately blocked up. Grass and earth had been stuffed into the overflow pipe and the reservoir tank was at risk of bursting. At court, Butler was fined 2 shillings for the charge of malicious damage. Gainey and Lair were discharged.[1]

Arthur's Well was situated opposite the entrance to Lovers Walk and along from Bank House on Bath Road. Sadly, the exact location is not marked today.

11th July 1968

---

1   *North Wilts Herald*, 7 August 1871.

This was the last serious flood of the high street, and it led to a dispute between Chippenham Town Council and the Bristol Avon River Authority (later subsumed into Wessex Water). Councillor Henry William Page believed that Ladyfield Brook was responsible for 80% of the flooded premises in Chippenham and improvements to the watercourse were needed to prevent a repeat. Engineer Frank Greenhalgh had little sympathy and blamed rubbish dumping. He argued that most of the flooding in the Foghamshire part of town was due to dumping in Hardenhuish Brook blocking its culverts. He was not prepared to recommend more work to be carried out for what he believed was an event likely to happen once in every 100,000 years.[1] Some residents supported this, citing the reason for flooding at 58 and

Flowers scrap dealers assist during the 1968 flood. Photograph - David Gearing.

60 Ladyfield Road, was due to the culvert where the brook ran under Ladyfield Road, becoming 'silted up' over time. This was partly due to rubbish being dumped in the brook which would then wash down and clog up the culvert.[2]

Clean sand was left behind after the water receded on the banks of the

1   *Chippenham News*, 2 August 1968.
2   Letter from EF Taylor, *Wiltshire Times* & News, 9 August 1968

river in Monkton Park which gave a look of sand dunes. Small shells were also present. This was several inches deep covering the fields at Westmead. Bulldozers had to be called in to move tonnes of sand. Hay that had swept along by the river and gathered in the fences had to be burnt.

Incomplete alterations made to Foghamshire did not consider drainage. The stream was still choked by rubble from the houses that were demolished there two years before.

The water reached the tops of the seats at the Astoria[1] and over 780 had to be ripped out of the bingo hall. A 140 gallon oil tank was swept from the cinema and ended up in the brook.

A charitable relief fund was set up by Mayor Arthur Evans. Over 240 homes were affected and a hundredweight of coal was given to all those seriously so.

Streets flooded included; Hill Rise, Westbrook Close, Foghamshire, Providence Terrace, Oaklands, Woodlands Road, Wessex Road, Honeybrook Close, Maple Way, Ladyfield Road, Palmer Street, Unity Street, Marshall Street, Loyalty Street, Park Lane, Patterdown, Westmead, St Mary Street, Lowden, Langley Road, Malmesbury Road and Sheldon Road.

Rain fell on the night of the 10th - 11th on already saturated ground. In 16 hours four inches of rain came down, which was an estimated 165 million gallons! Two or three times as much pushed into the area from outside.

More than 223 houses were involved in the flood, including 124 council houses. Over two tonnes of contaminated or flood damaged food had to be withdrawn from sale and sent to the council tip. The outdoor swimming pool had to be closed temporarily as it had also become contaminated.[2]

Steinbrook bridge in Kington Langley was washed away, where the road surface was seen to break apart like in an earthquake.[3]

Some of the houses in Foghamshire were flooded up to the downstairs ceiling.[4]

An elderly woman had to be rescued when she became trapped in a

1   *Chippenham News*, 19 July 1968.
2   *Chippenham News*, 26 July 1968.
3   *Wiltshire Times*, 12 July 1968.
4   *Wiltshire Times*, 12 July 1968.

flooded room in Tytherton Post Office.[1]

The small bridge in Audley Road was almost swept away. The new subway was flooded.[2]

By 3.40 the town centre was cut off. The co-operative could not move stock fast enough and thousands of pounds worth were lost.

George Flower's lorry was used as a ferry and was commended by police who estimated that thousands made use of this service. Town council workers gave up their holiday to work through, many working for 24 hours straight.

Rob Catt of the Bridge Centre provided a drying shed for the residents of Foghamshire, whilst also battling the floods at his youth club.

This was all despite the new bridge being built and sluice and river straightening work taking place to prevent such flooding!

12th July 1865

The election result was announced, with two Conservatives, Sir John Neeld and Sir Gabriel Goldney returned as Chippenham's MPs. This did not go down well with the townsfolk, most of whom were not eligible to vote, but supported the Liberal candidate, William Lysley.

Neeld and Goldney made speeches from the balcony of the Angel Hotel in front of a large, angry crowd. Some of their supporters heated pennies in the fire and threw them amongst the masses, who burnt their fingers when

The former King's Head boarded up. Currently back in use, as the Bargammon's Tavern board game cafe.

1   *Wiltshire Times*, 12 July 1968.
2   *Wiltshire Times*, 12 July 1968.

they tried to pick them up.

The 'mob' of around 500 men, women and children who had assembled, overpowered the police and smashed windows destroying property of the known Conservatives supporters in the town. *The Times* called it the 'palm of barbarism and brutality'. Tombstones were ripped out and thrown at the vicarage. One housebound occupant had, within quarter of an hour, fifty pound of stone thrown into their room, but protected by servants holding boards up around their bed.

Goldney was pursued across the Market Place to the King's Head where the landlady threw a bucket of dirty water on his pursuers. He then escaped to Monkton House via the Grove in St Mary Street, whilst the rioters retaliated. As the rioting intensified, a company of Coldstream Guards were sent for and their presence was required for three weeks.[1]

13th July 1935

The Cooperative Society butcher's stall. Postcard - Paula Champion

The £6000 extension to the Co-operative building was opened by Mayor William George Lenton, after nearly a year of reconstruction and remodelling of entire premises. The mayor was presented with

1   Chamberlain, J.A., (1976).

three inscribed bound volumes on the history of the Co-operative Society, as a memento of the occasion. The Women's Guild hosted a tea for the sixty or so delegates, in the Co-operative Hall after the ceremony.[1]

The society in Chippenham had grown from a single-roomed premises on the same site, which opened in 1889. There was significant local opposition to it at the time, presumably from other traders worried about being undercut by the more affordable prices. Additional buildings there were formally opened in 1909, with branches later established in Sheldon Road and London Road.

The 1935 improvements meant that instead of separate buildings in the high street, all three were merged, with some sections replaced or modified as required to form one large shop. Certain adaptations were made to lessen the impact of flood damage. Messrs Downing & Rudman we're contracted for the work with CWS of London subcontracted for the fixtures and fittings.[2]

14th July 1900

After a period of 'terrific heat', which led to several deaths in the area, the church clock at St Paul's began to behave in a bizarre manner. At midnight, rather than stopping after 12 strikes of the bell, it carried on an estimated 70 times! The following night, a midnight again, the strokes were 'numbered by hundreds.' The recorded temperature was 91 degrees Fahrenheit in the shade.[3]

15th July 1989

It was the official farewell to Westmead Infant and Junior Schools. The two schools opened for one last day, so that old pupils, staff and parents, could have a last look around. A party was held in the evening attended by 375 people and presentations were made to four of the teachers and a cleaner, who were also retiring; Joan Gingell, Myra Minns, Marion Bowerbank, Grace Punter and Lila Yeomans.

The last day of school was on 21 July. The pupils from the two

1   *North Wilts Herald*, 19 July 1935.
2   *Wiltshire Times*, 13 July 1935.
3   *Wiltshire Times*, 21 July 1900.

schools attended Kings Lodge at Pewsham in September.[1]

16th July 1913

Suffrage pilgrims on route to Hyde Park from Lands End reached Chippenham. This non-militant group were called Suffragists.[2]

The National Union of Women's Suffrage Societies (NUWSS) organised what was called 'The Great Suffrage Pilgrimage', which was supposed to be a peaceful demonstration.

When the group reached Chippenham from Corsham there were about 35 suffragists. A large crowd assembled in Market Place once news of their visit had spread. A conveyance was pulled up in front of the Bear Hotel which was used as a platform for speakers. Councillor Walters of Swindon introduced Miss Frances Sterling to a heckling crowd. He tried to reassure the crowd that these visitors did not support militant methods, and asked for them to be given a chance to have their say. It was estimated that 2-3000 people had arrived and they were not making things easy for the speakers. Walters reminded them that the women from the milk factory strike had been financially assisted by their organisation. When he sat down the crowd laughed.

As a second speaker set up from a motor car in front of the Waverley Restaurant, the crowd became more hostile and tried to overturn the first car in front of the Bear. The police surrounded it and backup came out from inside the Waverley. The ladies were escorted to a place of safety, through Arthur Spencer's Music Warehouse into Lords Lane and onto the Causeway.

Then the crowd turned their attention to a second group of suffragists in front of the fountain, but the police managed to get them into the car and away down the high street.

Advertisement for Spencer's Music Warehouse, 1933.

Once both meetings were broke up the disorder grew as it seemed that the crowd wanted the chance to heckle the suffragists more. An

1   *Wiltshire Times*, 21 July 1989.
2   *Civic Society Bulletin*, issue 149, August 2013.

anti-suffrage meeting led by Mrs Gladstone Solomon had occurred the night before outside Mr Spencer's and it was believed that the orchestra practising inside did so deliberately to make things difficult. It was suggested that the treatment of the suffragists was a retaliation.[1]

The situation had calmed the next day and a large crowd of supporters waved them off with their best wishes as they headed towards Calne.[2]

17th July 1643

After the Battle of Roundway Down on 13th, in which the Parliamentarians were defeated and 1800 taken prisoner, Waller escaped to Bristol. Many of the Roundheads briefly took refuge in Chippenham. William Iles of Stanley 'unwisely crossed their path' in St Mary Street so they killed him.

18th July 1894

The body of a newborn baby boy was found in a box at Ford. The discovery caused a 'great state of unwonted excitement' in the tiny hamlet. Elizabeth Hazell found the body in the house of an old man named John Hillier, and Ann Hillier, a 32-year-old paper finisher at Slaughterford Mills, who was accused of being the mother. The baby had a piece of tape wrapped around its neck but probably died of inattention rather than strangulation. Dr Wood of Corsham believed it was 'merciful' that the baby died, as it was 'malformed'. This offers some explanation as to why Ann Hillier neglected her baby, but as she was later taken to the workhouse at Chippenham, poverty may have also been a motive.[3]

Elizabeth Hazell is recorded on the 1891 census as a 'monthly nurse' which is an old term for midwife, and living at Dank's Down Cottage in Castle Combe.

19th July 1919

Peace Celebrations were held to celebrate the end of hostilities of the First World War, the Treaty of Versailles having been signed on 28 June 1919.

1   *Wiltshire Times*, 13 July 1913.
2   *Civic Society Bulletin*, issue 149, August 2013.
3   *Wiltshire County Advertiser*, 28 July 1894.

Peace Day service held in Market Place despite the inclement weather. Chippenham Museum Collection.

It was a rainy day in Chippenham but spirits were not dampened.

St Andrew's and St Paul's rang their bells in the early morning then a thanksgiving service attended by the mayor, was held in the market place. At 1pm, 450 discharged sailors and soldiers were given lunch in the Neeld Hall and afterwards 960 schoolchildren packed in the venue for a celebratory tea. Later that evening the hall hosted dancing.

A planned children's procession was abandoned because of the rain, but at 9pm there was a torchlight procession and a huge bonfire was set ablaze (as was the custom in Chippenham!).[1]

20th July 1907

It was a gloriously sunny day when King Edward VII, Queen Alexandra and Princess Victoria visited Chippenham, whilst on route to Bowood.

The centre of town was a 'sea of red, white and blue' with all the decorations put up to welcome them. A temporary grandstand filled an empty space between shops in the high street, formerly the site of a Tudor building used by Blackford's Ironmongers.[2] This is now 22-23 High Street, a grade II listed, four storey building built in 1908, currently home of Greggs and Julia's House charity shop.

1   *Western Daily Press*, 21 July 1920.
2   *Civic Society Bulletin*, Issue 99, Spring 2001, p.11

The King & Queen making their way to Bowood from Chippenham Railway Station, 1907.

The Royal Party cross the town bridge and approach the high street.

The Royal Party had a lucky escape on their return journey, whilst driving away from the town to Westonbirt, when a bolt of lightning struck the ground just in front of their car, hitting a tree.[1]

1   *Lloyd's Weekly*, 28 July 1907.

21st July 1896

An accident occurred at Messrs. Evans & O'Donnell's railway signal works, a forerunner of Westinghouse. Five men were 'seriously scalded' when a damp pipe was mistakenly placed in a tank containing molten metal.[1]

22nd July 1901

Florence Mary Stanley, a nurse probationer at Chippenham Workhouse, saw her fiancé off by train before drowning herself in the river. She had left a suicide note to her sweetheart named Newman, also of Chippenham, with the following words;

> A line to say goodbye. It cannot live longer, it is impossible. I am returning your bracelet, ring and brooch. Say goodbye to all in Chippenham for me. And now, darling, once again wishing you goodbye. Believe me, your broken-hearted lover, Florrie.

Her motive was a mystery as their relationship was not troubled. The verdict of the inquest was 'suicide while temporarily insane'.[2] A carpenter's daughter, Florence was 24 years old when she died. Her parents were Zebedee and Mary Stanley, who lived at Lowden, but were originally from Calne, where Florence was laid to rest three days later.

23rd July 1844

Joshua Barrett, a marble polisher from London, was travelling by train between Chippenham and Swindon at about 1pm. All of a sudden his hat blew out of the window and his immediate reaction was to jump from the carriage after it! As the train was moving, he was seriously hurt and eventually died of head injuries the next day. An inquest concluded with a verdict of accidental death. It seems that he had been drinking at the time.[3]

Joshua was buried at Langley Burrell Church on 26 July, close to his home in the village. He was 41.

---

1   *Northern Echo*, 22 July 1896.
2   *Weekly Mail*, 27 July 1901.
3   *Wiltshire Gazette*, 25 July 1844.

24th July 1939

Arthur Perry of Hawthorn Road placed a wire across the high street without taking reasonable precautions on behalf of his employers, Wessex Electricity Co. The wire was 15-16 feet off the ground between the Co-operative stores and the shop opposite, according to eyewitness Edward Bendry, an employee of Chippenham Town Council. At 9.30 am he watched as a lorry loaded with aeroplane wings struck the wire.

Perry was called out at midnight to attend an electrical breakdown at the Co-operative stores. When he resumed duty at 8 am he noticed the cable had sagged so went to get the ladders and equipment to fix the issue, placing a man on-site in case of high vehicles. The man was unfortunately taken away by another foreman just before the lorry with wings arrived.[1]

25th July 1948

It was the Annual Gaumont staff outing. A sports meeting was arranged by J Arthur Rank Organisation at Norbury, and a party of 28 attended from the Timber Street cinema. Sadly, the group arrived late so they had to just watch others take part in the sports activities. They were, however, kept busy by meeting film stars and collecting their autographs. These included; Margaret and her daughter 'Toots' Lockwood, Jean Simmons, Sid Field, Jack Warner and Richard Attenborough. Also, Sidney Bray, manager of the cinema, met and spent some time talking to Susan Shaw, who had visited Chippenham recently.[2]

26th July 1986

Cyril Downer shut his butcher's shop in Park Lane for the final time. Aged 80, he decided to retire after more than 40 years running the business single-handed, whilst also going out and delivering to customers throughout the area. His reputation as a quality butcher meant that customers would often let him choose their orders.

Mr Downer lived at Orchard Crescent off Hungerdown Lane and, once giving up his business, was able to spend more time at home with his wife and his pigeons. He was also a member of Chippenham Homing Society.[3]

1 *Wiltshire Times*, 30 September 1939.
2 *Wiltshire Times*, 31 July 1948.
3 *Gazette & Herald*, 31 July 1986.

27th July 1648

An ammunition convoy on route to Ireland rested in Chippenham.[1] The Borough records note that 'the Bailiff received three pounds for a nights feed for the horses' which were most likely kept at Westmead.

Presto supermarket (now Tesco) and the rear entrance to Emery Gate. Photograph - Tony White.

28th July 1986

Emery Gate Shopping Centre was officially opened by private ceremony to mark the completion of works; the first shoppers were able to visit from the following day. Only the Presto supermarket and a handful of other shops, were open from day one as most were still being fitted out.

These other shops were taken by; Dorothy Perkins, Southern Electricity Board, Billington's Super-save, Mortimer's, Professional Windows, Swindon Cheese Supplies, Dixons, BSC, Sassy Ltd, Allied Shoes, Bolloms, Peacocks Fashions, Chamberlain Wools and F Swift Butchers.

1   Goldney, p.62.

Building work was completed by North Wiltshire District Council in partnership with Beazer Projects Ltd.[1]

The new £7million shopping centre was immediately popular with customers. Rosemary Gartland, the wife of manager Tom Gartland, cut the ribbon when Presto Supermarket opened.[2]

29th July 2008

A 'mini tornado' hit Monkton Park during the afternoon. One man had a lucky escape after an 18ft tree was blown over as he was driving along Eastern Avenue, escaping with shock and bruises despite the tree flattening the back of the car.

The extreme weather event was centred only on Monkton Park with many matures trees being ripped up, as heavy rain and strong winds brought traffic to a standstill. A 60ft tree was blown over in the park itself along with several large trees at the adjacent Golf Club.

A 50ft high tree at Seymour House Care Home was smashed to pieces leaving branches hanging from the tree and damaging a fence and care home sign. The car park there was flooded by torrential rain.[3]

30th July 1925

Popular Headmaster Edward Thurston retired after 34 years at St Paul's Primary School. A public presentation was held and there was a large attendance of former and current scholars, staff and parents.

The school broke up on this day which was why it was

The Schoolmaster's House is all that remains of the original St Paul's School on Park Lane.

1   *Wiltshire Times* & News, 25 July 1986
2   *Wiltshire Times* & News, 1 August 1986
3   *Gazette & Herald*, 31 July 2008

chosen for the event; Thurston's actual retirement date wasn't until 31 August.

He was head of the boys school for 30 years and then the mixed school for four. There had been only two headmasters since the school was built in 1857. His replacement was Clement Penny who was trained in Calne.

Thurston received a gift of a gold watch, case of pipes and a fountain pen.

The watch had his initials and the following inscription;

> Presented to Mr E Thurston by the past and present scholars, the staff and the managers of St Paul's School upon his retirement after 34 years service - August 31, 1925.

Extracts were read from letters from ex-pupils who all spoke in high regard of Thurston. He thanked all for their kind words and for the presents, of which he said 'the watch would remind him of the flight of time, the chain of the links that bound them together, the pen to write to old scholars and others, and he could smoke the pipe of peace'. He said that 'he would not leave them as he would continue to live in the parish in which he has spent so many happy years'.

'Auld Lang Syne' and 'For He's a Jolly Good Fellow' were sung at the end of the event.[1]

31st July 1928

John Joyce of Preston near Milverton, Somerset, was summoned on a charge of dangerous driving near Chippenham on 31 July.

Gwendoline Matilda Lysley, wife of Major William Lowther Lysley of Pewsham House, was returning home, driven by a chauffeur, when a small car approached in the middle of the road. When it came close it turned towards her car, the chauffeur having to use a grass verge to avoid it. They turned around and followed it back to Chippenham War Memorial in Market Place, where the driver claimed she had the wrong person.

Joyce, a Somerset county councillor and justice of the peace, stated he had driven 50,000 miles in the car without an accident. He had

1   *Wiltshire Times*, 1 August 1925

been at a Shorthorn sale in Marlborough and claimed to be surprised when Mrs Lysley approached him. Joyce was found guilty but let off on payment of costs.[1]

AUGUST

1st August 1900

Winston Churchill visited Chippenham. At that time he was best known for his correspondent activities in the Boer War, but now he was hoping for a successful entry into politics. He attended a large gathering of Conservatives and Unionists in a field at the back of the Great Western Hotel where he defended the actions of the government and warned against the policies of the Liberals.[2]

A 'smart shower' of rain began just as he started to speak 'standing bare headed before the crowd' he remarked that if their gallant countrymen were facing Boer bullets in South Africa…surely they should not shrink from a few raindrops at home'.[3]

A few weeks later Churchill would win his first seat as an MP for Oldham and the Tories the 'Khaki Election' off the back of anticipated success in the war in South Africa.

2nd August 1792

Distinguished antiquary and author John Thorpe died in Chippenham and was buried at Hardenhuish Church.

3rd August 1901

A Requiem Mass for the fallen of the Boer War and the war in China was held at the Roman Catholic Church in St Mary's Place.

John Thorpe 1715-1792. Photo in the public domain.

1   *Western Daily Press*, 7 August 1928.
2   *Wiltshire Times*, 4 August 1900.
3   *Bath Chronicle*, 9 August 1900.

Caleb Slade had just returned from South Africa. Major Milsom, the former commandant of the Chippenham Volunteers presented Caleb with a street organ. Realising how lucky he was to return home unscathed he decided to use the instrument to raise money for those less fortunate. He walked the streets playing the organ and collected a 'nice little sum' for Mrs Haddrell, a widow of a former comrade killed at Springfontein, and for her four children.[1]

4th August 1930

The entries for the Chippenham Horse and Flower Show constituted a record. There were 1,700 entries from 253 exhibitors. The quality of entries were also the best received for the event. Despite uncertain weather, a crowd of around 15,000 attended.

As well as the horses on show, there were numerous tents filled with flowers, table decorations and fruit and vegetables.

Ellen White (wife of George Alfred Huelin White, solicitor and author), Mr Walter Glen, Mr Mortimer and Sir Daniel Cooper Bart. all from Chippenham, were among the prize winners.[2]

5th August 1943

Four men employed by Messrs Downing, Rudman & Bent were killed when an eight foot high wall toppled across a trench in which they were working to lay a sewer. All four were instantly crushed to death.

The wall stood in Foundry Lane and was fairly new, having been built only three years previously. It was found that the wall did not have adequate support as it wasn't strutted. Death from misadventure was recorded at the Coroner's inquest held at the Chippenham 'Institution'.

London Road Cemetery. The headstone of three Irishmen killed by a falling wall in Foundry Lane. A Scotsman who also died in the incident, was buried in an unmarked grave close by.

1   *Wiltshire Times*, 10 August 1901.
2   *Western Daily Press*, 5 August 1930.

Workmen of Downing, Rudman & Bent, c1950s. Derek Cook is second from left at the back. Photograph - Angela McQueen (Derek's daughter).

All four men were buried in London Road Cemetery. The headstone of the three Irishmen is still extant, 'erected by their comrades'. They are; Patrick Fraher, age 48 and James Connery, age 37, both of Tipperary and Maurice Flynn, age 36 of Waterford. Robert McClatchie, age 35 of Scotland, was buried in an unmarked grave close by.[1]

6th August 1948

It was the Funeral of Edgar Nelson Hibberd, age 52, who died at the Seaman's Hospital in Greenwich.[2] Nelson was taken ill in January while on a voyage to New Zealand and was brought back to England. In a bizarre coincidence his eldest brother, Joseph age 66, died a few hours before the ceremony, at his home at 39 Baydons Lane.

Another bizarre story relating to Nelson made the national newspapers in 1940. After being away from his home town, across the other side of the world for 21 years, Nelson Hibberd walked into the Three Crowns. His brother was in the pub at the time but neither

1   *Wiltshire Times*, 21 August 1943.
2   *Wiltshire Times*, 7 August 1948.

Nelson Hibberd's war medals which were found by Rikky Chace buried near a pond in July 2020 in Victoria, Australia.

recognised each other. He asked another patron if he knew any of the Hibberd family and the man pointed to Nelson's brother William. Whilst away, Nelson's parents had died so Bill took him to his sister's house and a family reunion was quickly arranged.

Nelson had joined the Navy in 1912 and served throughout the First World War. Whilst he was on leave in 1919 he transferred to the Australian Navy and wasn't seen again, his family had assumed he had died, as he hadn't been in contact for 10 years. He had been living rough in Australia, travelling over 8000 miles on foot to look for work, and did not want to contact the family until he had settled.[1]

7th August 1990

Sainsbury's opened their new supermarket on Bath Road at 9.30 am, the old store at Borough Parade was no longer large enough to meet customer demands, closing on August 4th.

The new store boasted 28 checkouts, Sketchleys one hour dry cleaning, parking for 586 cars and a petrol station next door. It took a year to build along with two new roundabouts and road improvements adjoining the site. Staff were transferred and some additionally taken on, to bring the total to 228.

1   *Daily Mirror*, 30 April 1940.

Sainsbury's in the town. Closed in 1990 moving out of town to Bath Road.

8th August 1905

William Stallard of Biddestone was spotted by PC Fred Wilmot, drunk, near the 'Reading Room' in the village. His wife was leading him by one hand whilst pushing their child along in a pram with the other. PC Wilmot also made note of Stallard's continual use of bad language. In his defence, he claimed to have previously suffered an accident and ever since a couple of pints of beer alone 'made him silly'. Stallard was fined 5s with a further 4s costs.

9th August 1916

'Loyalty Ward' opened at the Red Cross Hospital in the Neeld Hall, to add to 'Unity Ward' upstairs in the town hall next door. The opening ceremony was held in the evening. Mayor Townsend was present. A dedication service was conducted by Canon Maxwell-Gumbleton and Lady Margaret Spicer declared the ward open. This added provision for an additional 40 patients, doubling the capacity of the hospital. Within two weeks there were already 75 patients resident.

Patients on 'Unity Ward' at the town hall - from the Chippenham Museum Collection.

10th August 1892

The Chippenham & District Horticultural Society's Annual Exhibition, otherwise known as the Chippenham Flower Show, was held in the grounds of Hardenhuish Park. The band of the 1st Battalion Royal Inniskilling Fusiliers held a performance.[1] The weather was 'delightfully fine' and there were fairground attractions on the football ground. Fireworks, balloons and illuminations were provided by Pyrotechnist and Professor of Music, William Dee Penly of Wootton-under-Edge.

According to the advertisements beforehand, £150 in prizes were up for grabs. Sir John Dickson-Poynder MP was unable to attend owing to the fact he had caught a chill, so Edmund Henry Clutterbuck of Hardenhuish Park, presided in his place. Judges included gardeners of the local gentry; Thomas Challis (Earl of Pembroke, Wilton House), Alfred Read (The Neeld family at Grittleton House) and Thomas Nelson (Marquis de la Valette, Bowood).[2]

1   *North Wilts Herald*, 12 August 1892.
2   *Bath Chronicle*, 4 August 1892.

Programme of music from the Chippenham Horticultural Society's annual exhibition, 1892.

11th August 1930

General Sir Horace Lockwood Smith-Dorrien, the 'hero of the defence of Le Cateau', was injured in a car accident at a crossroads near Yatton Keynell, after visiting Biddestone Manor. Dr Ayres of Chippenham was sent for, and Sir Horace was taken to the cottage hospital, unconscious and with serious head injuries. He sadly died the next morning.

Sir Horace was the eleventh child from a well known west country family and educated at Harrow. After Sandhurst, he was commissioned into the Sherwood Foresters in 1876, with whom he spent his whole regimental career. His first active service was in the Zulu war and was one of the few who survived the massacre of the British at Isandhlwana.

After tours in Egypt, Sudan and South Africa he returned home, eventually rising to the highest possible position of Commander-in-Chief, succeeding Sir John French in 1907. The General led the Second Army during the early days of the First World War. He was Governor of

Gibraltar from 1918-1923, then retired after 48 years of service.[1]

12th August 1645

A Royalist raid, one of many during the Civil War, took place when Sir James Long from Devizes (leading a troop of calvary and 50 infantry) and Colonel Boville from Lacock (40 Musketeers along with 20 calvary under Major Cooke), joined up to force their way into the town. Fighting took place in Foghamshire and St Mary Street. They successfully seized a quantity of ammunition and horses.[2]

The garrison at Chippenham was under the command of Lieutenant Colonel William Eyres, and most of its cavalry were absent. There were light defences along Causeway and London Road consisting of two banks of earth. The outer with a narrow passage and the inner with no way through. Next to the town bridge was a wooden turnpike fitted with spikes. Major Francis Dowett and Captain Williams led 20 infantry against the turnpike on the Town Bridge approach whilst Long, Boville and Cooke took the calvary across the river to attack the barricades on the end of the causeway.

Boville's men quickly took the first of the earthworks but struggled with the second. They took shelter in some houses overlooking the barricade and gave enough covering fire for Long's calvary to charge it and then continue along the causeway into the market place.

The remaining members of the garrison defending the turnpike were now attacked from both sides and put up strong resistance before falling back and allowing Dowett and the infantry in.

Eyres tried defend the town with his remaining 240 men, with no less than four counter attacks, but were eventually routed by the Royalists. After losing a dozen men, the parliamentarians fled along St Mary Street. Twelve were killed and several drowned trying to escape across the river.

After two hours of fighting the Royalists lost four men including Cornet Dowett, Major Dowett's brother. They had 80 taken prisoner including Colonel Eyres. It was the last significant Royalist success of the whole war.[3]

---

1   *Wiltshire Times*, 16 August 1930.
2   Chamberlain, p.55.
3   CSB, No.142, November 2011.

13th August 1942

At the town hall, Austrian Dr Franz Burger gave a talk on his experiences as an escapee from a German concentration camp. Alderman Edward Newall Tuck and Mayor Edmund Portman Awdry hosted a capacity audience. The Ministry of Information event described the horrors of the concentration camps including the harsh treatment, executions and gas chambers.

Dr Burger had two spells in the camps because of his anti-Nazi views. He wanted to warn of the danger the Nazis posed to the English.[1]

14th August 1877

Chippenham Amateur Swimming Club was founded at its first committee meeting, held in The Bear Hotel. A year later, the club acquired land off what is now Long Close adjacent to the River Avon. Part of the river was cordoned off with a floating boom to form a 'pool'. This was condemned by the local authority in 1948 when bathing in the Avon was consider unsafe due to pollution. The club then began to travel to Devizes until the outdoor pool at Monkton Park opened in 1960.

Chippenham Amateur Swimming Club badge, c1960s. Photograph - David Else.

Initially christened 'The Chippenham Swimming Club', it's still running today and is one of the oldest swimming clubs in the country.

15th August 1945

VJ Day celebrations were not as large as those on VE Day, in most Wiltshire towns. Chippenham however bucked the trend. When news of the surrender came through on the Tuesday night, thousands took to the streets playing hooters, car horns, whistles, drums and tins. The partying went on through the night, in some parts not finishing until sunrise.

1 *Wiltshire Times*, 22 August 1942.

On Wednesday morning, flags and bunting were hung around the town, just like on VE Day, and fairy lights lit up the town bridge and nearby riverbanks. In the evening the large crowds returned to the streets and the King's Speech was relayed in the market place, where the people sang and danced. Many attended thanksgiving services.

Some of the residential streets had their own bonfires and dancing. King Alfred Street, for example, brought out rugs and deckchairs and sat around their fire late into the night.[1]

16th August 1908

Reginald Baker, Arthur Boyes and Walter Tavinor were accused of cruelty towards a Poodle belonging to Captain Cookson of 'The Palace', which was walking in London Road.

The young men had their own Fox Terriers and a Retriever which they set on the Poodle.

Tavinor was seen to also throw a stone that hit the Poodle, but he claimed that he threw it to try and separate the dogs. Robert Brooks and Lot Webb of 65 and 67 London Road respectively, witnessed the whole incident and supported the prosecution by the Society for the Prevention of Cruelty to Animals. Frank Britten, Henry Day and Joseph Pearce gave evidence to support the defence. In the end, the accused were each fined 5s.[2]

17th August 1886

William Higgins, a tinman of Chippenham was caught taking fish from the river near to the milk factory on this night. He was summoned to the Petty Sessions by William Watts, water bailiff, where he happily admitted the act, but argued he had every right to fish there.[3]

William was listed as a tinplate worker or ironmonger on censuses and lived at The Bridge. 'Higgins' on the Bridge' was so named after him.

18th August 2020

There was a Spitfire flypast over Chippenham Hospital just after 2pm. This was arranged to honour the work of the NHS staff during the

---

1   *Wiltshire Times*, 18 August 1945.
2   *Wiltshire Times*, 5 September 1908.
3   *Wilts & Gloucestershire Standard*, 4 September 1886.

Covid-19 pandemic. 'THANK U NHS' was written on the underside of the wings of the plane. When it reached Chippenham it circled three times before flying on to Trowbridge Hospital.

19th August 1968

At St Peter's Church, a 50 foot spire was hoisted into place as the building work for the new church came to an end. It was manufactured using glass-reinforced plastic with copper added for colour. The shape was a 10-foot wide hexagonal dome with six 36-foot high struts supporting a 14-foot cross.

The 'THANK U NHS' Spitfire flying over Chippenham Hospital. Photograph - Dave Stone.

Made in Yeovil, it was assembled at the factory first then taken apart and reassembled on-site at Lords Mead. The one-ton structure was then lifted into place by a 50-ton crane in just nine minutes.

This spire was briefly taken down in 1980 because it had been leaking. The legs needed fixing and the lantern had to be replaced.[1] It was sent to Weston Super Mare where fibreglass experts Concargo Ltd made the repairs.[2]

A bell was also added in the recess above the main entrance. This came from All Saints, Clifton which suffered severe bomb damage in the blitz on 2 December 1940. The vicar of All Saints was a close friend of St Peter's vicar, Rev Terence Simper, and bell was a link between the two churches.

The bell was inscribed 'AJ Turner, London 1866'.[3] It was donated by All Saints as it was not needed when the church was rebuilt.

Three men, one of whom had worked on the site, stole the bell from the hut of contractors Dudley Coles Long, broke it up and took it to a scrap merchant in Bristol. After they were caught, the culprits had to repay for the re-founding of the bell in instalments.

1 *Gazette & Herald*, 28 August 1980
2 *Chippenham News*, 22 August 1980
3 *Wiltshire Times*, 15 March 1968.

St Peter's Church, Lords Mead.

It cost £70,000 to build the church. Money was raised from appeals and war damage claims made for bombed churches subsequently not rebuilt. The Bishop of Bristol laid the foundation stone on 27 June 1967 and the Bishop of Malmesbury consecrated the site on 7 December 1968. Most of the 'impressive modern interior' is the work of artist and sculptor Frank Roper, a student of Henry Moore.

20th August 1897

Dr Joseph William Furey, a 'locum tenens' to Dr William Thomas Briscoe of Chippenham, was taken to the Royal United Hospital in Bath, due to the 'shocking' injuries he received as a result of a trap accident whilst being driven along Parliament Street by Dr Briscoe's groom, Henry Sartain.

On their way into town the horse bolted. Dr Furey jumped out of the vehicle but unfortunately landed on some spiked railings at the front of John Kirby's earthenware dealership at Prospect House (67 Parliament Street). One spike entered his throat, fracturing his jaw and another into one of his arms. He was conscious but could not speak, but still managed to write a self-diagnosis on slips of paper!

The horse, which then survived running the trap into a ditch, seems to have had a history of accidents. It had previously bolted and threw Dr Briscoe himself off in the high street and in April 1895 was transporting Dr George Watson, when he fell off and died.[2] Watson was a native of Strichen, Aberdeenshire and only 27 years of age.[3]

21st August 1943

Queen Mary visited Chippenham and stopped at Joe Buckle's fishmonger shop to inspect his collection of 600 old fire insurance office signs, known as 'firemarks'.[4] Buckle's shop was in a fine Tudor building that used to stand in the high street on the corner of River Street.

On Queen Mary's arrival, two airmen stepped out of the car first. They were Leading Aircraftman Pinder and Aircraftman 1st class Wildman. She had noticed them walking into town so stopped and offered them a lift, something which she was well known for doing for service personnel. They didn't realise who she was until they were greeted by a cheering crowd on their arrival into town and as she presented both with a souvenir medallion with her monogram, another of her traditions.

Joe Buckle with Queen Mary outside his shop. Photograph - Chippenham Museum Collection.

1   *Cambrian News & Merionethshire Standard,* 27 August 1897.
2   *Wiltshire Times,* 28 August 1897.
3   *Aberdeen Press & Journal,* 17 May 1895.
4   *The Times,* 24 August 1943.

22nd August 1832

A public dinner was held to celebrate the passing of the Reform Bill. Approximately 2,000 of the town's poorest people were treated to a roast beef dinner, followed by plum pudding, washed down with strong beer. For this event to take place, 68 tables were set up in the town centre. During the build-up to the meal, the people assembled in Englands, then walked into town with music and flag-waving. The celebrations ended with a bonfire (as was customary in Chippenham) and fireworks.

23rd August 1965

At the telephone exchange, an 18-year-old employee was suspended on full pay pending completion of an inquiry. She was one of two women at the exchange who reportedly gave statements to the Wiltshire Echo newspaper, describing how calls, including some made by the Royal Family, were regularly listened to by operators.

The other woman, aged 20, had already resigned and found a job as a barmaid. The Post Office headquarters investigation branch looked into the allegations that telephone calls were frequently and consistently

The Telephone Exchange on Cocklebury Road opposite Chippenham Station.

tapped at the Chippenham exchange.

Queen Elizabeth the Queen Mother was the most frequent royal visitor to the district, staying at Spye Park with Captain Frank and Lady Avice Spicer, each year for the Cheltenham Gold Cup meeting. The Queen and members of her family often stayed at Badminton, the seat of the Duke of Beaufort.

The staff were later cleared as the investigators were not able to find any evidence to substantiate the allegation that any conversations had become public knowledge. However, the freelance journalist who supplied the story claimed that a whitewashing campaign by the Post Office covered up the truth. He argued that both girls had proof of others listening in and divulging conversations, but were not prepared to give names because of the Official Secrets Act.[1]

24th August 1899

A fire broke out shortly before 1 am at the Rose & Crown in Market Place. PC Hillier had passed through Lords Lane about 20 minutes earlier and noticed nothing, but when he got to the town bridge he could see the flames reflecting on the water.

The Rose & Crown in Market Place.

Part of the building and the stables ran in a southernly direction behind Francis William Belcher's draper shop and the Five Alls. One part of this went over the yard and joined to Mr Brinkworth's coal wharf forming a loft used as a skittle alley. It was here that the fire began and both the skittle alley and stable were destroyed by the fire. The horses were rescued in time, one having his mane singed by the flames.

Water was pumped from the nearby canal by the fire brigade and both Rose & Crown and the Five Alls were saved from destruction.

1   *The Times*, 2 September 1965.

Mr and Mrs Morse, their seven children, a servant and the Bird family who were visiting, were all in the Rose & Crown but managed to escape.

Mrs Baker, the wife of the Five Alls landlord however, was in such a state of shock, that she cried out 'Oh, I shall die!' then promptly collapsed and died. She had lately been having problems with her heart.

Those living nearby had awoken to hear what they thought was the patting of raindrops, Chippenham having been experiencing a drought for some time. It seems what they actually heard were crackles from the fire.[1]

25th August 1951

As part of the the Festival of Britain programme, an 'All Services Tattoo' was held in Monkton Park, during far from ideal weather conditions. A combination of regulars, national servicemen and cadets took part.

Trumpeters of the Royal Wiltshire Yeomanry opened the programme that included a motorcycle riding display by the Army Mechanical Transport School and a physical training demonstration by national servicemen from the Royal Army Pay Corps Training Centre in Devizes.

A much anticipated demonstration by Sea Cadet Frogman Ian Francis had to be called off because of a defective suit.[2]

26th August 1860

Shortly after 10pm, the Tetbury Mail Cart was passing through the town, when for some reason the horse ran into the River Avon. Due to the height of the water, both horse and cart were pulled under the bridge. The driver, William Henry Gurney of Tetbury, tried to jump to the bank of 'Mr Wilson's Island', but did not make it. By the time his cries for help were heard and acted on, it was too late; he had been swept away. The horse and cart were both pulled from the river at Back Avon Bridge, but despite lengthy attempts, Gurney's body was not found for some time.[3] William was later buried in Tetbury on 4 September age 27.[4]

1   *Wiltshire Times*, 26 August 1899.
2   *Wiltshire Times*, 1 September 1951
3   *Reading Mercury*, 1 September 1860.
4   Gloucestershire, England, Church of England Burials, 1813–1988

27th August 1938

Having just turned 65, Joseph William Eaton of 4 Ricardo Road retired after almost 50 years with the Great Western Railway, 42 years of which was as a porter at Chippenham station. He served under five station masters. Many alterations to the station buildings, including the removal of the fully covered roof, occurred during his time there.[1] Joseph was originally from Acton Turville and as a boy worked the stables as a groom at Badminton for the Duke of Beaufort. He married in 1897 in Alderton, not far from Acton Turville and he almost certainly met his wife at Badminton House where she was a housemaid. To stay local, they moved to Chippenham where Joseph became a porter. He was earning 17s when he started which had risen to 24s by 1913.[2]

Joseph Eaton sitting at Chippenham Railway Station with colleagues stood behind. Photograph - Di & Mike Eaton

28th August 1882

Captain William Sutton of the Salvation Army was charged with causing an obstruction near the Western Arches. The Army had assembled near the Three Crowns where they held an open-air service,

1   *Wiltshire Times*, 13 August 1938.
2   Information from Joseph Eaton's Grandson, 31 August 2021.

then they marched to the barracks, which at that time was under one of the arches of the railway viaduct. When arriving opposite the gates, they stopped for about 20 minutes, where they, and an angry mob who were following them, blocked the road to all traffic. Sutton was then asked to take his followers inside, but he argued that they were being stopped from doing so by the mob itself. The police disagreed and he was arrested.

In court, despite the Salvation Army producing 11 witnesses who could say that the mob blocked the road, Sutton was found guilty of obstruction and told to pay a fine of 50 shillings or face gaol by default.[1]

Baptist minister Henry Bayley Bardwell, 1842-1917. Supported the Salvation Army during their establishment in the town. Photograph - Sue Ievy

The witnesses also reported that the harassment of the Salvation Army during their activities was a regular occurrence. Sutton at first tried to appeal, and then refused to pay the fine. After a hearing which lasted four hours, he was sent to Devizes Gaol. A few days later his fine had been paid and he was collected by Henry Bayley Bardwell, a Baptist minister of Orwell House, who accompanied him back to Chippenham by train, where he received heroes welcome. A large crowd greeted him, the Salvation Army band played and he was escorted back to the barracks.[2]

29th August 2009

Chippenham River Festival was relaunched after an absence dating back to 1968. The free event, which was held over the August bank holiday weekend, was hailed, by its organisers, as the 'biggest family fun day to hit the town in decades.' It was organised by the Chippenham &

1   *Wilts & Gloucestershire Standard*, 23 September 1882
2   *Bath Chronicle*, 28 September 1882.

Patrick Geoghegan in what was the last Chippenham River Festival in 1968 (top, far left) and his son Daniel Geoghegan in its revival in 2009 (bottom, front left). Photograph - Daniel Geoghegan.

Villages Area Partnership and Wiltshire Vale Rotary Club, with support from Wiltshire Council and numerous sponsors.

Dragon boat races, riverboat trips, live bands, river swimming, a sailing club exhibition, an angling masterclass, Punch and Judy show and a Hercules flypast were among the attractions.[1]

30th August 1987

Secretary of State for Northern Ireland, Tom King, was the target of a suspected IRA assassination plot. King lived at Ford near

1   Advertisement.

Chippenham. Two suspects were arrested on the grounds of his home and a third later at a campsite close to Wookey Hole.[1] They were then held for eight days without charge, as permitted under the Prevention of Terrorism Act, at Chippenham Police Station.[2]

In October of the following year, John McCann, Finbar Cullen and Martina Shanahan, all from the Republic of Ireland, were convicted at Winchester Crown Court of conspiracy to murder and sent to prison for 25 years. On 27 April 1990 this sentence was quashed and the 'Winchester Three' were released.[3]

31st August 1890

'Important to Railway Men' and 'Six days shalt thou labour' were headings on flyers handed out at the Temperance Hall meeting arranged by the Amalgamated Society of Railway Servants. Liberal and Baptist minister Rev Henry Bayley Bardwell presided.

1917, May - First ever joint trade union demonstration in Chippenham, which raised funds for the Cottage Hospital. The National Union for Railwaymen leading down Station Hill. Photograph - Paula Champion.

1 *Wiltshire Times* & *News*, 4 September 1987.
2 *Los Angeles Times*, 8 September 1987.
3 Northern Ireland history, www.news.bbc.co.uk, 18 March 1999.

With 12 hour days being worked, a reduction to a 10 hour day with overtime pay was a moderate demand from the society. Conditions for railway workers had improved but there were still social, well-being and mental health concerns and reported neglect of families. Company directors did not want to have talks with the society so the hope was that the shareholders could be engaged with instead. It was resolved to form a Chippenham branch of the ASRS and many of those in attendance agreed to sign up.[1]

In 1913 the ASRS merged with other railway worker unions, forming the National Union of Railwaymen.

SEPTEMBER

1st September 1996

The two Methodist churches joined as one at Monkton Hill. The last service at the Causeway was on 25 August 1996. The cost of repairs and renewals there had become too much. There were problems with the

The Central Methodist Church on Monkton Hill. The original site of the Black Horse public house.

1   *Devizes and Wiltshire Gazette*, 4 September 1890.

heating in the church and schoolroom. The closure of the Causeway was 'devastating' for its members.

The building has since been used as a music and arts centre.

2nd September 1983

Gale force winds and heavy rain began and lasted until 4 September. Winds reached 128.8km/h in some areas. Southern England took the brunt of the gales. Thomas Hope, 53, of Hertfordshire, was driving a flatbed trailer carrying a Caterpillar tractor along Bristol Road. He was instantly killed when a tree split in two, with half of the trunk falling onto his cab as he passed Chippenham Town's football ground, heading towards towards Bristol.[1]

3rd September 1891

In the early hours, after several days of declining health, Sir John Neeld died at Grittleton House, age 86. Only a few days previously he had attended the Grittleton Flower Show and appeared on top form saying; 'I am an old man, but I am not tired of life'. He died of dropsy. Sir John was the brother of Joseph Neeld, who he took over the family estate from, after he died in 1856.

Sir John was Treasurer of Chippenham Savings Bank and donated land for the building of the Jubilee Institute in Market Place. He was buried in the family vault in Leigh Delamere church.[2]

4th September 1967

A suspected UFO or Flying Saucer appeared in the field of Dick Jennings at Elm Tree Farm, Patterdown. It was discovered by the farmer at around 9.30 am.

There were six, every 30 miles from the next, in a straight line across the south of England. They contained a strange gooey liquid, batteries, a transmitter and a loudspeaker device. The others were found at Clevedon, Newbury, Ascot, Bromley and Queensborough.

The Chippenham 'saucer' was dealt with by an Army Bomb Disposal Unit, who carried out a controlled explosion after moving it to a rubbish

---

1 *The Times*, 3 September 1983.
2 *North Wilts Herald*, 4 September 1891.

tip. All that was left was a sludgy, smelly mess.[1]

Police at the 'landing sites' across the country were left baffled. It was clear early on that they were made in England and not outer space, but by who and why, was the big mystery.

Each 'craft' was small (4ft x 3ft) and gun-metal in colour. A dome on top was made of fibreglass and the bottom section contained a rancid mixture of flour and water. They made a beeping noise when tilted. The one in Chippenham hissed and footprints were found leading up to it. At some of the other sites, eyewitnesses reported flashing lights in the sky, even though the whole event was later revealed to be a hoax.

The 'Flying Saucers' before their journey began. Photograph - Roger Palmer.

Christopher Southall, age 21, an apprentice at the Royal Aircraft Establishment, Farnborough claimed responsibility working with students from Farnborough Technical College. He said he was convinced that the real thing will visit one day, so thought it a good idea to test the police and experts.[2]

5th September 1934

Tragedy was narrowly averted when a three year old boy fell 20 feet from a wall into the River Avon. His hero was Arthur Farmer of Factory Lane (now Westmead Lane) who was best known at the time for his prowess on the pitch for Chippenham Town Football Club. Farmer had been unemployed for six months since coming home from Singapore where he served with the 1st Wiltshire Regiment.

The child, Reginald Howell, also of Factory Lane, was playing in the cattle pens in the Market Yard. He climbed up a wall which backed onto the river, but lost his balance and fell. Farmer was passing through the

1 *Birmingham Daily Post*, 5 September 1967.
2 *The Times*, 5 September 1967.

yard when he heard the cries of other children. With no hesitation, he jumped in the river and pulled out little Reggie who was miraculously unscathed despite his ordeal.¹

Sadly, in the summer of 1939, Reggie went missing one evening after playing in the river at Westmead. Now 8 years old and even though he was experienced with the dangers of the water, history repeated itself. Unfortunately, no one witnessed what happened. His clothes were discovered, half an hour after he had gone missing, by the Baker brothers of Timber Street.

Four day later his body was found 50 yards from the spot he was last seen. The depth of the water varied at the 'Sandy Beach' from two feet, to holes up to fourteen feet deep. According to the testimony of 9 year old Alan Bishop of 36 Factory Lane at the inquest, up to 50-60 children regularly played at the beach, avoiding the hazardous part known by locals as 'The Rock Hole'.²

Reggie Howell, who was rescued from the river by Arthur Farmer. Photograph - George & Doreen Howell

6th September 1939

Cecily May Poulett Wallace, a relation of the Duke of Beaufort, sold Pew Hill House to Westinghouse. They initially used it for their war time head office, before it returned to London in 1946. Then it was used as living accommodation for ex service personnel until 1959, when it became a hostel for the company's apprentices; an estimated 550 passing through up to 1981. In July 1982, it once again became used as head office.

1   *North Wilts Herald*, 7 September 1934.
2   *Wiltshire Times*, 17 June 1939

ON THIS DAY

A Westinghouse letterhead from 1935, before the head office moved to Pew Hill House.

This was a replacement Pew Hill House built for a Miss Dickson in the 'Maverick Tudor & Stuart' style. The original building stood here, from c1773, to when fire partially destroyed it on 22 January 1894. Although the damage wasn't too extensive, it was demolished and rebuilt in 1895. The original was the home of Thomas Pocock, woollen cloth manufacturer at Waterford Mills.[12]

7th September 1822

A riot took place between men from Chippenham and of the Langleys. There are at least two accounts of how it began, the first was recounted by Rev John Jeremiah Daniell. Some offence was given at a Langley Fitzurse (Kington Langley) village revel by a group of young men from Chippenham. Around 10.30 on this day, 30-40 men armed with bludgeons, marched into town. Constables and the men of the town tried to drive them out but the constables were 'beaten down'. Two men died and 31 men, women and children were injured. At the following Lent Assizes in 1823, it was found that both parties were equally to blame. One Langley man was taken ill whilst dancing at the Bear Inn, and began to fit. Pushing and fighting then began when more Langley men arrived in support of their friends. Sticks and stones flew as the violence spread along the high street and up New Road. No individual could be proven as to have taken part, so all were released!

Another account described that the fighting began where the Western Arches are now, at the junction of Marshfield Road and New Road,

1   Benson, 1982.
2   1851 census.

The Western Arches is believed to be built on the site of where the 1822 Chippenham Riot began.

carried on through Foghamshire, The Ivy and Back Avon Bridge then on to Bath Road.

Joseph Hull, a Saddler of the high street, was found dead at the bottom of St Paul Street. James Reynolds was also killed, his body being found at the entrance of the Lovers Walk footpath between Bath Road and Back Avon Bridge. Joseph Moore, Bailiff and High Constable, lost his left eye. In total; two died, 11 people were severely and 19 slightly wounded.

Kilvert mentions the riot in his diary entry for 4 February 1873. He was told that it was 'the fault of Chippenham who started it.' The Langley men entered the town that day having had enough of their ill treatment in Chippenham on market days.

The Coroners inquest brought a verdict of wilful murder and riot. The evidence collated for the trial against the main aggressors covered '60 sides of foolscap paper.'[1]

At the Lent Assizes in 1823, six men were tried on the charge of riot. They were; John Matthews and Henry Knight (the alleged ringleaders), James Isaac, Benjamin Salter Junior, John Thomas and Harry Gardner. Another five men were charged with murder. They were; George Thomas, James Mountjoy, Thomas Pearce, John Woodman and William Bryant. All eleven men were found not guilty.

1   *Kentish Weekly Post*, 20 September 1823.

8th September 1831

To commemorate the coronation of King William the Fourth and Queen Adelaide, twenty guineas were given to the poor of Chippenham. Children of the National, Sunday and all other charity schools in the town, were treated to a sit down dinner. Later, a bonfire was lit in the market place.[1]

9th September 1898

A tragic accident occurred under the railway arch at the bottom of Rowden Hill. Charles Kelson was walking in front of a traction engine, guiding the driver as a pilot. George Whiting, the driver of the engine, had warned Kelson not to walk too close to its front, but as they passed through the arch, Whiting felt the engine go over something. Albert Ritchins, whose job was to steer the engine, didn't see Kelson as he was looking back up Rowden Hill to be sure nothing was approaching. Kelson's leg was crushed and needed to be amputated, but he didn't survive the injury. An inquest held at the workhouse later returned a verdict of 'accidental death'.[2]

Charles Kelson was the son of William James and Mary Ann Kelson and was buried on 20 September 1898 at London Road Cemetery.

10th September 2000

Safeway (now Morrisons) at Cepen Park North. Photograph - James Lutener.

1   Goldney, p.156.
2   *Bristol Mercury*, 24 September 1898.

An anonymous caller caused chaos in Chippenham by claiming a bomb was about to explode at the Cepen Park Safeway supermarket. Fortunately, this was a hoax, but police took the threat very seriously, evacuating the area and closing surrounding roads. Traffic was diverted onto the bypass leading to tailbacks during the nine-hour operation. The Army bomb disposal team were recruited to carry out a series of controlled explosions on a suspicious vehicle in the car park. Fortunately, no explosive device was found.[1]

11th September 1988

The long-awaited £2.5million inner relief road, the Avenue La Flèche, opened and 'Two-Way Day' took place, converting the one-way traffic system back to two way. New mini roundabouts were put in to replace traffic lights at the New Road and Station Hill junction and by the Town Bridge. A leaflet was delivered to all households to explain the changes and yellow signs were placed along the routes to give advanced notice.[2]

The opening of the Avenue La Flèche on 11th September 1988 by Councillor Jack Ainslie, Chairman of Wiltshire County Council along with the Mayor of La Flèche Jean Virlogeux. Photograph - John Scragg

Days later it became apparent that not many were using the new 'bypass' road. Only two out of every ten drivers heading to Calne or Devizes were avoiding the queues in New Road. Drivers took some time to get used to the new two-way traffic system and crossing points.

The opening didn't go off without a hitch. The VIP double-decker bus got stuck in the New Road traffic and red-faced officials had to quickly reassure their guests that it was due to other roadworks and not because of the new road.

Chippenham Mayor Ray Anscombe and La Flèche Mayor Jean Virlogeaux, who travelled to the UK specifically for the ceremony, joined Wiltshire County Council Chairman Jack Ainslie who officiated the ceremony.

1   *Gazette & Herald*, 14 September 2000.
2   *Wiltshire Times* & News, 2 September 1988.

Avenue La Flèche under construction. Photograph - Tim Fortune.

The first person to journey on the new road was cyclist Margaret Bassett. She expressed disappointment at the lack of a cycle lane.

Work on the 1.5 km road had begun in February 1987. The most difficult part was building a new bridge over the River Avon, but despite this, the road was finished two months ahead of schedule by Westbury based firm AE Farr.[1]

12th September 1850

There was a grand public dinner held in honour of Joseph Neeld and as thanks for his gift to the town, of a recently completed extension to the cheese and cattle market. This included a new market room, extended market yard and extra buildings.

The town celebrated this gift with the ringing of bells, firing of cannon, bands of music and by decorating the streets and houses, much like at a jubilee celebration. Neeld entered the town from his seat in Grittleton, with a procession of the workmen who had built the extension, an assembly of local clergymen, and his tenants on horseback.

All political feelings were 'thrown aside' as a euphoric atmosphere spread through the town. Such was the gratitude of the people, some

---

1   *Wiltshire Times* & News, 16 September 1988.

even wanted to release Neeld's horses and draw his carriage themselves! Neeld would not accept.

At 5pm nearly 500 people 'of all ranks' sat down to dinner in the new shed, which was 156 feet long.

Neeld's philanthropic gesture was made possible due to a large inherited fortune.[1]

The London Illustrated News sent a reporter and artist to attend. Over 400 tons of cheese were 'pitched', overflowing into the high street.

13th September 1955

On the outskirts of town, at Sheldon Farm, lightning struck a Dutch barn. An adjoining shed caught alight and two cows inside sadly died. The strike also set fire to the electricity supply pole and knocked down a farmworker.[2]

14th September 2016

Plans for a distribution centre for The Range were finally denied by Wiltshire Council after nearly two years of planning consent wrangling. The company had hoped to build on land north of the A350 Cepen Way near the Morrison's roundabout. Many locals objected to the size and location, whilst just as many welcomed the plans because of the promise of the creation of 1000 jobs.

Protestors gather to oppose The Range. Photograph - Brian Mathew.

1 *Devizes Gazette*, 19 September 1850.
2 *The Times*, 14 September 1955.

Another stumbling block for The Range's plan was the presence of the remains of a Roman villa close by.

The company had already given up their plan by this date and began looking into a new site near Bristol, but the application was still open and campaigners were waiting for a redevelopment of the site to be abandoned completely.[1]

15th September 1859

Isambard Kingdom Brunel died ten days after suffering a stroke whilst working onboard the SS Great Eastern. Chippenham was one of many places which can thank him for rushing it into the age of steam.

Brunel's works office, which he used whilst his Great Western Railway was built through the town, is preserved in the railway station car park.

Brunel's Western Arches and Western Villas (demolished and replaced with the DWP office tower) were also his work. The Brunel Pub now surrounds Orwell House. This was where Brunel stayed when it was the home of Rowland Brotherhood and his family. Brotherhood was a friend and business partner of Brunel's.

16th September 1927

A serious flood occurred on this day. Ironically it had already been designated as a 'Lifeboat Day', which was a fundraising event organised by the RNLI. The town bridge became impassable due to four feet of water, which caused trading to cease, including at the big monthly market. The Bristol to London bus could not get past Chippenham. Despite all this, a 'band of undismayed women' were able to sell 'Lifeboat' flags.[2]

Back Avon Bridge was washed away and never replaced.

A total of £13 14s was collected which was only £3 10s less than the previous year. This was despite the fact that the town market had been cancelled so less people were in the town, showing that the flood itself must have illustrated the need for such a charity and its work.[3]

1 *Gazette & Herald*, 14 September 2016.
2 *Guardian*, 17 September 1927.
3 *The Lifeboat, Journal of the RNLI*, November 1927.

Flood of September, 1927. Chippenham Museum Collection.

17th September 1926

An 'egg dealer' from London, William Francis Humphreys, obstructed the highway in the market place. Humphreys claimed that he had parked his car to the side of Smallcombe's shop, as was correct and had paid a toll to leave it there. He said that someone must have pushed his car into the road. The toll collector, Harry Milsom, had no record that Humphreys had paid a toll and even if he had seen the car parked where Humphreys claimed, he would have asked the police to move it. At court, Humphreys was found to have caused an obstruction and fined 2s 6d.[1]

18th September 1965

The last passenger train ran on the Chippenham to Calne branch line, affectionately known as the 'Calne Bunk'.

Geoff Taylor sounded the Last Post as the last train drew into

---

1   *Wiltshire Times*, 6 November 1926.

Calne station. Booking Clerk Kathleen Williamson issued the first ticket from the Calne Booking Office opened during WW2 and was there to issue the last on that day. Driver Frank Cannon and Passenger Guard Freddie Bond manned the train for the last journey, carrying more than 200 people including the mayor and mayoress of Calne. Fireworks were let off.[1]

Passenger and Westinghouse employee Mr Gordon Smith, who had been using the service for over 40 years and raised a petition to prevent its closure, described the railway as a 'Golden Four Miles'. He was one of the last passengers that day and was presented by a signalman's lamp by the area manager of British Rail, Mr W J Pike.

The last train back from Calne, 1965. Photograph - David Gearing.

Don Lovelock, the son of a former Black Dog Halt stationmaster, made sound tape recordings of the final journey there, and Len Cockell of Calne, did the same from Chippenham to Calne and back on the train.

The track was lifted in 1967.[2] The metal bridge over the River Avon was removed in 1971, due to its decay, leaving it too unsafe to remain. A footbridge was installed here c2002 and is still known as the 'Black Bridge' by locals, the original wooden bridge being painted black.

There was hope that a mile long section of the line between Black Dog Halt and Calne could be saved by rail enthusiasts for running steam locomotives, but in the end it wasn't to be.[3]

1   *Bath Chronicle* 20 September 1965
2   *The Calne Branch*, Tanner, 1972.
3   *Chippenham News*, 24 September 1965.

19th September 1903

At the town bridge end of Bath Road, stands the former Salvation Army Citadel, on the corner next to the Oxfam charity shop. The foundation stones were laid by Frank Fields and Sir John Goldney on this date. A large number of people attended the stone laying ceremony. 17 stones were laid in total. The last two were by Frank Fields and Major Byers. Afterwards, a public tea to celebrate was held at the Temperance Hall.[1]

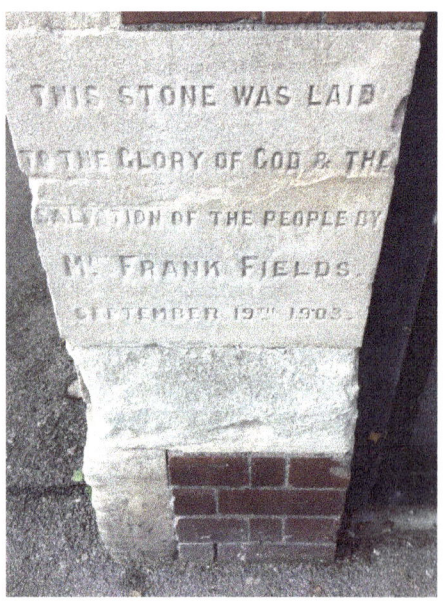

Foundation Stone from The Citadel, Bath Road.

Previously, the Army had been meeting in a corrugated iron structure on the same site. The Army purchased the freehold and the old building was donated to the Wesleyan's for a mission hall at Woodlands. This was re-erected by Mr Frank Fields. The cost was £35, including seats. The building was 54 feet long by 23 feet wide and could seat 220. It was known as the 'Wesley Hall.' The opening service took place on Wednesday 28 October 1903.

20th September 1934

An estimated £300 of damage was caused by a mystery fire, that destroyed three cars at Victor Langley's garage in St Mary Street. The cars belonged to Reginald Escott, Wilfred Archard and Frederick Mackness and they were stored in a shed next to Prospect Place. Only 25 minutes after Escott put his car in the shed, Mrs Holly of 25 St Mary Street could see the reflection of the flames in the sky. Her son Wilfred ran to the fire station, while her two daughters Ethel and Kathleen raised the alarm with the neighbours, including a fireman called Albert Smith who fortuitously lived nearby.

1   *North Wilts Herald,* 25 September 1903.

Langley moved his garage to the corner of Audley Road and Gastons Road. This would later become Seagers Coaches and MOT Centre.

21st September 1971

Shortly before 4pm, an out of control lorry crashed through a wall and hedge at Greentops, 28 Hardenhuish Lane, directly opposite the vehicular exit for Hardenhuish School. The quick thinking of the driver, Peter Marsden, prevented a serious tragedy by turning the lorry away from the pavement full of school pupils who had just finished for the day. He managed to steer towards the other side of the road and narrowly avoided injury himself. The lorry was carrying a load of talcum powder. Brake failure was believed to be the cause of the accident.[1]

22nd September 1858

A Testimonial Dinner was held at the Bear Inn in honour of William Nicholls, organised by the dairy farmers and cheese manufacturers of the area. The Mayor, Jacob Phillips, chaired proceedings and discussed how Nicholls had benefitted the industry with his invention of Fluid Extract of Annatto. This was used as a colouring for cheese to give its yellow appearance. Previously it was produced in a 'cake' form but Nicholls had produced a far superior product, which was soon adopted by the Cheddar cheesemakers and further afield. Nicholls was presented with a silver tea and coffee 'equipage' with the following inscription on the coffee pot;

Fragment of pottery discovered in the old canal channel at the top of the Avenue La Flèche when the roundabout was being built. Photograph - Michael Slater of westcountrybottles.co.uk

1 *Gazette & Herald*, 23 September 1971

PROGRAMME 3d.

CHIPPENHAM TOWN SPORTS CLUB

ATHLETIC SPORTS MEETING

(Under A.A.A. and W.A.A.A. Laws and N.C.U. Rules)

Chippenham Sports Ground, Marshfield Road,

Saturday, September 23rd, 1944.

First Event 2 p.m.   Gates Open 1.15 p.m.

NO BETTING ALLOWED.

The Open Foot Events at this Meeting are framed by the A.A.A. Board of Handicappers up to and including 16th Sept., 1944.
W. G. STONE, A.A.A. Official Handicapper.

The Open Cycle Handicaps at this Meeting are framed from the N.C.U. Champion and made up to and including Sept. 16th, 1944.   E. A. WARBUTTON, Official Handicapper.

Event No. 1.   100 yards Boys 10—14.   Final
  First............................   Time............................

Event No. 2.   100 yards Girls 10—14.   Final
  First................Second...............Time........

Event No. 3.   100 yards Lads 16—19.   Final
  First............Second...........Third..............
  Time............ Time............... Time..............

Event No. 4.   100 yards Ladies—Open.   Final
  First............Second...........Third..............
  Time............ Time............... Time..............

Event No. 5.   School Girls Relay.   Final
  First............................   Time............................

Programme from an Athletic Sports Meeting held during the Second World War.

Presented to Mr William Nicholls, by the dairy farmers, cheesefactors, and other friends, as a mark of respect, and to mark the deep sense entertained by them, of his indefatigable perseverance in the successful production of the invaluable preparation so essential for colouring cheese, 'The Fluid Extract of Annatto' - September 1858.[1]

23rd September 1944

An 'Athletic Sports Meeting' was held at Chippenham Town Sports Club, with David Eccles MP presenting the team prizes. The majority of the events held were for women and children, this was probably because most fit and able men were engaged in some kind of war work, therefore unable to take part, although there was a Mens Tug-of-War included in the programme.

24th September 1932

A 'vanishing tramp' saved Derry Hill Reserves village football team from defeat. After walking 25 miles that day, the unknown visitor had been resting under a hedge by the football field. Short on players, the fixture was about to be called off, when he was asked to help. The man admitted he hadn't kicked a ball in five years, but agreed. There was a surprised look on the faces of the Lowden FC players when they met nine men and a 'rather battered looking spectator of about 35'.[2] He was wearing trousers and worn boots, which hardly gave him an advantage against the other players.[3] However, one of the visiting Lowden players was reported to have said 'he didn't need to run around us, he could walk through us'.[4] He went on to score three magnificent goals to make the game a draw, and was to be rewarded for his services after Derry Hill passed a cap round, but by then the man had vanished.[5]

25th September 1897

The Liberal Club opened. It was named after Prime Minister William Ewart Gladstone. A smoking concert was held following a public meeting. The naming was done with the blessing of the 'grand old man'

1 *Devizes and Wiltshire Gazette*, 30 September 1858.
2 *Daily Herald*, 28 September 1932.
3 *Belfast Telegraph*, 29 September 1932.
4 *North Wilts Herald*, 30 September 1932.
5 *Daily Herald*, 28 September 1932.

The Gladstone Liberal Club, 2020. Empty, but soon to be converted into flats.

Gladstone himself. He wrote; 'I am very sensible of the high compliment which the Liberals of Chippenham propose to pay me, disabled as I am by age and circumstances, from the performance of practical duty'.

Originally, the Liberal Club opened in St Mary Street in 1895, then soon after moved to the Market Place, but again needed a new home as the 'coffee palace' acquired part of this premises. Parts of the new club buildings, formerly a stable, were used for a bowling alley.

26th September 1858

What was described as an 'extraordinary something' was seen floating in the air over Chippenham. Some described it as looking like 'half a collapsed balloon.' This led to the most plausible explanation being that it belonged to Mr Godard, a famous balloonist, known as an 'aeronaut' at the time. He had made an ascent from the Paris Hippodrome on the Thursday before but something went wrong and he had to cut the balloon free from its carriage.

27th September 1869

Dr William Henry Colborne died aged only 47, leaving a wife and seven children. The cause of death was exhaustion whilst suffering from typhoid fever. For the previous couple of years he had been overworked and anxious.

He was known for his kindness, philanthropy and sense of civic duty and was due to take on the role of mayor in November.

> A more kindly disposed and amiable man - a man more full of anxiety for his patients - more charitable to the poor, both with purse and medicine, more ready to help them to the attainment of health and contentment by the warm interest he took in all that concerned them - never lived.

William graduated from the University of London in 1853 having already joined his father's established practice in Chippenham. His father, William senior, had only recently passed away himself in 1868.

Colborne was house surgeon to Robert Liston, who was famous for his fast operations and pioneering use of ether as an anaesthetic.[1]

28th September 1935

A bore-hole was drilled at Ivy Fields in order to start pumping a new water supply for the expanding town. At a simple ceremony, Mayor

A view of Ivy Fields before the waterworks were established and the Charter Road housing estate was built.

1   *The British Medical Journal*, 16 October 1869.

William George Lenton, opened the valve to start the flow of water. This needed to be left running for two weeks before the Ministry of Health could sanction the new waterworks. It was estimated that six million gallons were wasted during that fortnight. Town Surveyor Albert Edward Adams chose the site and calculated that it could supply water to 20,000 inhabitants. The source is 20 feet higher than the river flood level so there was no chance of contamination by river water. The bore-hole went 150 feet deep. It was proven that the other supplies at Westmead and at Chippenham Laundry, derived from the same source, because the water level in those fell during the excessive test pumping at Ivy Fields.

29th September 1945

For a month from this date, a Henry III copy of the Magna Carta, was available for the public to view at Lacock Abbey. This was thanks to Miss Matilda Theresa Talbot, who refused offers from private individuals for the document, and instead passed it to the British Museum. She had already recently given the abbey estate and village to the National Trust.

The copy, dated 1225, was secretly buried during the war for safety. It was thought to have been taken to the abbey in 1232, by the abbey's foundress, Ela, Countess of Salisbury.

In 1940, with the threat of invasion, Miss Talbot wrapped the document and the leather case in which it had been kept for many years in flannel, and had it soldered into a zinc case. She buried it under the floor of her air-raid shelter, with only her sister and two workmen, sworn to secrecy, knowing where it was.[1]

Deborah Cox (left) and her manager June Blackford are presented to HRH Princess Anne. Photograph - Deborah Etherington.

30th September 1983

Princess Anne opened the new headquarters and factory of Wavin Plastics at Parsonage Way. Her Royal Highness was given a

1   *The Times*, 20 September 1945.

tour by the Lord-Lieutenant for Wiltshire, Colonel Hugh Brassey and Mr Chappell head of the company.[1] She received a gift on behalf of the Save the Children Fund, of which she has been president since 1970, for £75,000, which was represented by a piece of pipe, 100 tons of which were to be sent to third world countries for improvement of water supplies. Six year old Morag Goodwin, whose father George was systems and information manager, presented a bouquet to the princess.

Maud Heath, East Tytherton and Langley Fitzurse primary schools were invited to wave flags and attend a free lunch to celebrate the event.[2]

OCTOBER

1st October 1874

George Rourke Bryant of Pocock's, at Waterford Mills in Factory Lane, Woollen Manufacturers, patented a more efficient way of washing

Workers at Waterford Mill in Factory Lane (now Westmead Lane), c1910. Left to right: back row - J Wheeler, G Turk, D Tucker, A Wheeler, G Phillips, 2nd row: Miss N Wootton, Mrs Bristow, Mrs Wheeler, Mr Wheeler, Mr Crook, Mr Pope, Mr Ryall, H Beaven, M Townsend, Mr H Tucker, A Brewer, 3rd row: Miss E Hunt, Mrs S Howell, Miss Duckett, Miss L Hillman, Miss F Balch, Miss E Hillman, Miss F Short, Miss R Davis, foreman, Mr E Porter, front row: Miss Skuse, Mr S Fry, Mr W Scott, Mr A Denning, Mr F Cook, Miss Lily Hancock (sister of Florence Hancock). Photograph - Ron Challinor.

1   *The Times*, 1 October 1983.
2   *Bath & West Evening Chronicle*, 1 October 1983.

wool. His invention of 'Improved machinery for washing wool' was entered into the Commissioners of Patents Journal, as Patent no 3364.

His idea was that by increasing the speed and economy of the washing of wool, the machine would remain relatively dry and more could be quickly loaded for the next wash.

2nd October 1901

An arriving mail train was found with a door open on a third class carriage. Two passengers were inside when leaving Bath, but at Chippenham, only one sleeping passenger was found. After a search of the line, the body of Dr Reid Crow was discovered two miles away. He had travelled from South Africa to Plymouth and was on route back to Paddington when the tragedy occurred.[1]

David Reid Crow was Assistant Colonial Surgeon in the Gold Coast Colony (Ghana, from independence in 1957). He practiced in London but was originally from Edinburgh. He was returning from a Government appointment in Ashanti. He was single aged 33 years old. The other passenger, Henry Albert Hart, had returned from Africa with Dr Crow, meeting up on the ship back to Plymouth. On the train after supper they both fell asleep. When he was awoke at Chippenham, Dr Crow was gone. Guard Thomas Henry Adlam discovered the open door with Hatt asleep inside. On discovery of Dr Crow it was found that death would have been instantaneous as his neck was broken. There were no signs of a struggle so a verdict of accidental death was given at the following inquest.

A 3rd Class one way ticket from Paddington to Chippenham.

3rd October 2000

The 'Millennium Wall' was unveiled by HRH the Duchess of Gloucester GCVO at Westmead. She was reported to have been rather bemused to declare a wall 'open'.[2] The purpose of the wall was to 'give a glimpse of how children saw their world at the start of the third millennium AD.

---

1   *Rhyl Record & Advertiser*, 12 October 1901.
2   *Civic Society Bulletin*, issue 98, Winter, 2000

A section of the Millennium Wall at Westmead.

All children age 12 and under from the 13 Chippenham schools had the opportunity to design the tiles which decorated the wall. A blue line runs across the wall representing the River Avon which is close by. Mayor Sandie Webb officiated on this very wet and gloomy day.

There are 4000 tiles in total divided into 13 themes, one for each school;

Agriculture - Hardenhuish, Industry - Ivy Lane, Railways & Canals - St Nick's, People & Personalities - Sheldon, Education - Queen's Crescent, Cultures - Monkton Park, Religion - St Mary's, Buildings - St Paul's, Historical - Charter, Markets & Fairs - St Peter's, Transport - Redlands, Future - Frogwell, Environment & World - King's Lodge.

4th October 1724

The Reverend Robert Cock died at the age of 57. He bequeathed £50, all of his money, for teaching 'poor girls' to read and for 'instruction in the knowledge and practice of the Christian religion'. A field at Hardenhuish was purchased with this money so that the rental income could be used for this purpose. It is the only known attempt to start a national school until 1824.[1]

1   Daniell, p.103.

A memorial to Robert Cock can be found in the north chapel of St Andrew's Church.

5th October 1897

Henry Shell, a baker of Oldfield Park, Bath, had been suffering from depression and had been staying with his wife's family in Chippenham, hoping the change would do him some good.

When David Gordon Fuller left Chippenham station driving the 5.50am goods train to Salisbury, he saw Henry standing on the embankment ahead. As he got closer Shell threw off his hat and led down on the rails. Fuller's best efforts to stop were in vain. Henry was taken to Bath hospital where he became violent and delirious. He died from shock related to his horrific injuries. He was only 27 years old and left behind a widow, Annie Shell.[1]

6th October 1951

Ronald Maura Dryden overturned and crashed at 'Camp Corner' on the first lap of the 500cc Formula 3 car heat of the Castle Combe National Race Meeting. He was at the wheel of a JBS Norton works car, manufactured by James Bottoms and Son Ltd. Dryden suffered head injuries in the crash, on the final bend of the circuit. Sadly, he died in an ambulance along Lodge Road, on the way to Cossham Memorial Hospital in Bristol. He was 42.

Ronald was quite bald from a young age, after the shock of an earlier accident, which was why he chose his ironic nickname 'Curly'. An RAF Squadron Leader during the Second World War, he survived being shot down over the North Sea. When he wasn't racing, Dryden was landlord of the George Hotel at Dorchester-on-Thames, near Oxford.[2,3]

7th October 1899

The foundation stone of the Chippenham and District Secondary and Technical School at Cocklebury Road was laid by Lady Dickson-Poynder.

1   *Bristol Times & Mirror*, 9 October 1897.
2   www.motorsportmemorial.org
3   www.historicracing.com

The total cost of the build was £6,021 9s. 1d. Of this, £1,170 17s. was paid from public subscription and £700 from Colborne's charity.[1] Messrs Smith & Light carried out the work.

A large assembly was present for the occasion, including Mayor Alderman John Coles, the town clerk (who was also secretary of the school), Robert Edwin Brinkworth (architect), Mr and Mrs Newall Tuck, Canon Rich and various members of the Goldney, Awdry and Lysley families.

Chippenham and District Secondary and Technical School, Cocklebury Road.

An acre of land was taken from the Monkton Estate facing Cocklebury Road. The reason for this choice of location was because of its pleasant surroundings and close proximity to the railway station. Many boys from Corsham attended the school and the idea was that they could go home for lunch and be back for lessons at 2pm.

Lady Poynder, wife of Chippenham MP Sir John Dickson-Poynder, was presented with a silver trowel at the laying of the foundation stone and said; 'I have much pleasure in laying this stone, and at the same time, of cementing it with my good wishes.'

Fees of £4 10s a year and 10 scholarship places were made available.[2]

1   Chamberlain, J.A., (1976), p.102.
2   *Wiltshire Times*, 14 October 1899.

8th October 1918

Captain Wallace Mortimer Rooke of the Royal Wiltshire Yeomanry, died due to the Spanish influenza, caught whilst serving in France. His family lived at The Ivy, off Bath Road. Aged 28, Wallace was attached to 2nd Wilts after the start of the war and was 'mentioned in despatches' for service above the call of duty.

He was buried with military honours, and the band of the Wiltshire Regiment lead the cortège to London Road cemetery. Three volleys were fired over the coffin, which was draped in the Union Flag.

Tragedy struck twice more for the family when Rooke's sisters both passed away, also of the Spanish Flu, within days of each other on 14 (Doris age 17) and 16 October (Ellen age 20). The sisters were both nurses at the Neeld Red Cross hospital.

London Road Cemetery. The grave of three Rooke family members who succumbed to Spanish Flu in 1918.

It appears that Rooke brought the virus back from France and despite initially recovering, relapsed and likely passed on the virus to his sisters.[1]

9th October 1961

The frontage of a former jewellers which adjoined the Post Office in Market Place began to slip away from its retaining ties. This was during its conversion into a coach booking office. High winds and heavy rain caused eight inches of movement during the previous night.

Workmen were required to demolish the shop front to make it safe, but whilst this was taking place, the main route through the town had to be closed. All London bound traffic on the A4, including heavy lorries and buses, had to wind their way through St Mary Street, the original coaching route.[2]

1 *Wiltshire Times,* 19 October 1918.
2 *Bath Chronicle,* 16 October 1961.

10th October 1986

Fr John Desmond Millett, age 55, prevented a suicide attempt on the Western Arches in July, and on this day received an award from Wiltshire Police for his bravery. He had recently gone under the knife for major heart surgery, but did not hesitate to climb up the 60ft slope to help the man.

PC Cornock and Chief Inspector Tamlyn tried to no avail to persuade the man to come down. After two hours he asked to speak to Fr Millett, who was able to talk him round in five minutes. He was then helped down and taken to hospital for treatment.

The incident almost ended in disaster though, when the man nearly slipped over the edge, but the policemen managed to grab hold in time. They too received bravery awards.[1]

Fr Millett, later becoming a Canon, was the incumbent parish priest for Chippenham up until his death in 2021. Born in Clonmell, Ireland in 1930, he was originally a teacher, but answered his calling to study for the priesthood in 1967.

Alderman Keary wearing the mayoral chain of office.

11th October 1900

Alderman Alfred John Keary died at the foot of the steps outside the town hall. He had just left the building after recording his vote. Keary was Chippenham's mayor four times; in 1879, 1882, 1884 and 1889.[2]

There is a brass inscription in St Andrew's church which reads;

To the glory of God and in memory of Alfred John Keary born September 23 1832 died at Chippenham October 11 1900 Greatly beloved and deeply lamented Requiescat in Pace

1   *Gazette & Herald*, 16 October 1986.
2   *Evening Express*, 11 October 1900.

Keary was a solicitor and partner in the firm of Keary, Stokes and Goldney. He and his family were mentioned as social acquaintances several times in Kilvert's diary. Alfred's Father, William Keary, was originally from Galway.

After his funeral service at St Andrew's, the glass hearse and mourners were led along the Causeway and London Road and to the borough boundary by tradesmen and council members. From there he was taken to Tytherton for the internment, the final resting place of his infant daughter Nora.

As a mark of respect, the flag on the town hall was flown at half mast, and from 1.30, all business was suspended until after the funeral. Joe Buckle was one of the pallbearers.[1]

12th October 1910

On a 'miserably wet day' the Public Hall and Skating Rink was opened on Station Hill by Lady Margaret Spicer of Spye Park. Sid Martin, champion fancy skater of England, gave a demonstration on the skate

The former skating hall on Station Hill is now a Dorothy House Hospice charity furniture shop.

1   *Wiltshire Times*, 20 October 1900.

floor and was soon accompanied by the other guests at the ceremony. A bouquet was presented to Lady Spicer by little Miss 'Bobs' Holland.

Built using Hartham Park stone, with a 100 foot long roof lantern for light and ventilation, the hall had a capacity for 1500 people and cost between £4,000 and £5,000. Chippenham had been disadvantaged up until then compared to other towns, as it did not have such a large hall for various uses of business or pleasure. Despite the fact that the skating craze may have been short lived, there were many other functions that the hall could accommodate, being 150ft long and 75ft wide, including dances, concerts and cinematography.[1]

13th October 1986

It was the official switching on of Chippenham Town Football Club's new floodlights. A friendly match was held against Swindon Town who respectfully brought eight of their first team players. It was hoped the gate receipts would go some way to repaying the cost of the installation.

Chairman Doug Webb thanked Lou Macari for bringing his Fourth Division Champions to Chippenham and for fielding a strong squad. Although Swindon beat Chippenham, at that time playing in the Great Mills League, 3-1, Chippenham striker Dave Grant scored a memorable goal in front of the home crowd of 800 spectators.

Other fundraising activities organised included a sponsored walk and an auction of donated souvenirs from Football League clubs.

The cost of the floodlights was £11,000. Labour was free as club members, including vice chairman Ken Brewer, dug out the holes and erected the lights themselves.[2]

14th October 1936

Around 6am in the morning, the mutilated body of a man was discovered on the line about a mile from Chippenham Railway Station, in the direction of Swindon. Signalman Hall was finishing his shift at the Langley Signal Box, when he found him.

The unfortunate man was Charles William Tomes of 76 King's Hill Road, Swindon. He worked in the Breeze Block Shop at Messrs Bradley & Sons. At the inquest at St Paul's Church Hall, two mysteries

1   *North Wilts Herald*, 14 October 1910.
2   *Gazette & Herald*, 16 October 1986.

Cocklebury Bridge crossing the railway tracks just outside Chippenham towards Swindon.

were unsolved surrounding the death of 30 year old Charles. Why his damaged motorcycle was found 300 yards from the top of Pew Hill lying on the side of the road and why this was 24 hours before he was found by Alfred James Ball, Signalman for Great Western Railway. His brother told the inquest that Charles had been suffering from 'nerves' due to his strenuous job and he advised him to see a doctor. Charles may have had an accident and in confusion went on the railway via the access by Cocklebury Lane.[1]

15th October 1952

At No 1 Air Navigation School, RAF Hullavington, a Wellington aircraft veered off the runway during take off, hit a hangar and blew up. Four people were killed. The explosion was heard across neighbouring villages but was not seen due to the thick fog, which was the only possible cause of the crash found during the following inquest.[2]

The pilot was Sgt Norman Pain of Trowbridge. The other crew members were Flt Sgt Leonard Hodges, Acting Pilot Officers John

1   *Wiltshire Times*, 14 October 1899.
2   *Wiltshire Times*, 18 October 1952.

Phillip and Anthony Saunders, the latter of which rests in Chippenham Cemetery.[1]

16th October 1905

Lacock Halt opened approximately 2-3 miles from Chippenham Railway Station, on the line from Thingley Junction to Westbury, at the point where the road to Corsham crosses the line.

It was half a mile from the village, as when the line was originally built, there was local opposition to it so Great Western Railway moved the line further away from its original plan. Over the years, the villagers could see the benefits of the railway and unsuccessfully petitioned for a station after all. The change came with the introduction of the new motor rail cars.

The first trip to Lacock from Chippenham was supposed to leave just after 10am but due to a snapped valve, the rail car broke down after half a mile at Patterdown. An engine was used to push the car onto Trowbridge but it meant that the first train to use the station was half an hour late.

A return ticket from Lacock Halt to Chippenham.

Two weeks earlier, the running of local services between Chippenham and Trowbridge were taken over by steam rail-motors to reduce operational costs. Lacock Halt was opened with the aim of increasing passenger traffic. The platforms at Lacock were about 100 feet in length with basic shelters provided. It closed on 16 April 1966 as part of the Beeching Cuts.

17th October 1943

A Civil Defence exercise took place in Chippenham. These were important to ensure volunteers were ready for any potential incident

1   pro-patria.co.uk

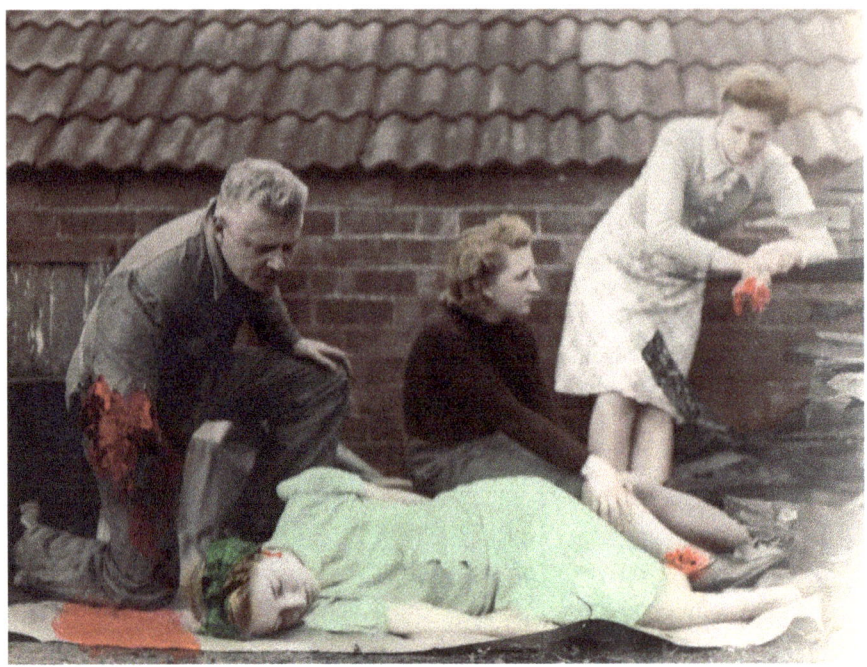

First Aid Practice. The 'patients' are; Mr WH Weston (shattered arm), Sylvia Webb (fractured skull), Grace Hawkins (crushed hand) and Mary Gibbs (fractured leg). Photograph - Jean Morrison.

that could arise during the war. The Red Cross and St John Ambulance members took part and were able to demonstrate their first aid skills.

18th October 1901

Whilst excavating the foundations of a new workshop, men at the Signal Works discovered the remains of a an adult male skeleton. The skull and teeth were particularly well preserved and it was found in a crumpled position under where a hedge used to run. All traces of clothing had gone. One theory of its origin, is that of a navvy employed in the 1840s, when the railway was under construction, less than 100 yards away from the burial site.[1]

19th October 1886

St Peter's Church opened in Lowden. It was built to accommodate up to 250 people, on land adjacent to Elizabeth Utterson's Almshouses,

1   *Wiltshire Times*, 19 October 1901.

which were built in 1884. The foundation stone was laid on 20 July 1885 by Canon Rich and is under the east window of the church.[1]

Its intended purpose, was to act as a mission chapel for Lowden, Rowden and Sheldon, which at that time consisted of about 200 homes and 1000 people. The total cost of the build was £1095, and was designed by architect Graham Awdry of Westminster, who was also responsible for the five almshouses, which are of similar style. Messrs Smith & Light of Chippenham were the builders.

A view of St Peter's Church, Lowden, taken from the railway line. Utterson's Almshouses are to the right.

20th October 2015

The former Middlefield Adult Training Centre in Hungerdown Lane collapsed due to the severity of a large fire. The fire service were called into action shortly after 3pm. Thankfully, the building was empty. The next day three girls were arrested on suspicion of arson.[2]

The site was due to be sold off by Wiltshire Council with part of the site going to the Order of St John's Trust for a new care home. The centre was eventually demolished and a Lidl supermarket and houses have built in its place.

1 Chamberlain, J.A., (1976), p.38.
2 *Gazette & Herald*, 28 October 2015.

The former Middlefield Adult Education Centre is destroyed by fire. Photograph - Chris Dunster.

21st October 1896

The opening and dedication service was held at the new Methodist church in the Causeway. The Rev William Jones, President of the Primitive Methodist Conference (or Head of the Church) officiated. Mayor Charles Robert Stevens was in attendance. The Rev Alfred Warcup was the incumbent minister.

Building work had completed quickly as the foundation stone laying event only took place a few months before on 3 June. The new church replaced the Friends (Quakers) Meeting House purchased in 1832, which carried on being used as the Methodist Schoolroom.[1]

The Primitive Methodist Church on the Causeway closed in 1996

1   Causeway Methodist Church Diamond Jubilee Year, souvenir handbook, 1956.

22nd October 1991

On the M4 motorway near Chippenham, police caught a Fiat Croma and a Rover 827 speeding at 100 mph. At first they thought the two cars were racing but were shocked to discover a 13-foot tow rope between them. Horrified mechanic Jonathan Griffith was in the Rover and was pleased when the police stopped them. Still shaking, Griffith told PC Andrew Alexander that 'people would pay a lot of money to experience a fairground ride like what he had experienced'. They were on route from Bridgend to London for gearbox repairs. The driver was charged with reckless driving, speeding and towing a vehicle in the outside lane.[1]

23rd October 1963

The idea of a museum in Chippenham was first recorded in 1909 when Aldermen John Stevens and John Coles suggested that the Yelde Hall should be used as one, but it wasn't until 1963 that this came to fruition.[2] The concept was largely conceived however, by Aldermen Herbert Arthur Cruse and Edward Newall Tuck, along with local historian Dr Arnold Platts. Sadly, all three died before their vision became a reality.

The first incarnation of Chippenham Museum was opened in the Yelde Hall by Mayor Gertrude Emmeline Moss. In the first week of being open, it attracted 259 visitors. Joseph Chamberlain was the first honorary curator, the last was Tam Pearce. Chippenham College lecturer and archaeologist Mike Stone was the first full time manager.[3]

The Yelde has had many uses over the centuries. Possibly a market hall until the 1580s when shops and shambles began to be built close by. The main purpose was for a court house and civic meetings. There was a lockup going back as far as the 13th century. It is not known for sure how long a hall has been on the site. It was home of Chippenham Savings Bank from 1822 to 1846. Then it was used as an armoury for the Wiltshire Regiment Volunteer Rifle Corps from 1846 to 1911, when it moved to The Ivy. From 1870 it was the home of the Chippenham Fire

---

1   *Guardian* 24 October 1991.
2   *Bristol Evening Post*, 26 June 1963.
3   *Civic Society Bulletin*, issue 95, Spring 2000

Brigade, before their move to Dallas Road in 1945. After this, the hall was gradually updated to allow use as the town's museum.

The Yelde Hall during its Chippenham Fire Brigade days.

24th-25th October 1882

Believed to be the 'greatest' flood on record at Chippenham. Three inches of rain fell in 24 hours. By 11am the water has started to spill from the river into the high street at 'the usual spot' near Messrs Pond's store. Some shopkeepers tried to stop the waters entering their premises using planks, but this only worked for a short time. Mr William Milsom, builder, installed a temporary bridge alongside the pavement over the town bridge, charging a halfpenny a crossing. At 2pm, 'Milsom's Bridge' swept away as the river began to rise at an alarming rate. By 4pm the town mill and Foghamshire were also flooded. Some people who passed through the town almost lost their lives. At 7.45pm, with the waters still rising, Police Superintendent Barrett gave orders for crossings to cease. The landlord of the Little George, Thomas Hall, was charging sixpence a trip, but at 8.15 he was told by Barrett 'you are not to come through anymore tonight. If you get through alright call at the Police Station and tell my wife I shall not be home tonight.' As Hall made this final crossing, the water came up through the floor of the wagon and the horses had to swim the deepest part.[1] Albert and Herbert Powell, Mr Harcombe and John Hetherington were the last passengers. At 11pm, the level was 14 feet and 2 inches above normal, with the deepest part of the high street being 5ft. When John Singer's shop flooded, a barrel of treacle floated downstream and washed up in River Street which 'provided a fine feast for the lads there'. Occupants of shops on The Bridge were evacuated to Greenway Farm. Back Avon Bridge was under reconstruction by John Jones of Langley Road Foundry at the time and new piers and foundations were swept away. An eight-ton tree trunk washed down from Monkton Park stuck under the town bridge but eventually shot out the other side. The gate posts at the entrance to The Ivy were also washed away.

Two nine-gallon casks of Oakhill Porter was washed away from the town and were happily received near to Lacock by some lucky finders! Lacock itself was one of many villages along the river who suffered from the flood waters.[2]

25th October 1942

Lady Superintendent-in-Chief Edwina Mountbatten of the St John Ambulance visited the town. She inspected members of the Chippenham Nursing Division, along with the Corsham St John Ambulance, at the Co-operative Hall in Foghamshire. This was a special occasion and Lady Edwina made sure she spoke to almost all 80 members attending the parade.

26th October 1929

An important day in the history of the Scout movement in Chippenham. Mayor Fred Hart Porter opened a new hall for the 1st Chippenham Boy Scouts at Audley Road.

The Scout group was formed in 1911 and its previous headquarters was a small Army hut just above the new one. Despite having no scoutmaster at the time, the troop were going from strength to strength, even winning the 'County Totem Pole' at the last competition and were holders of the shield for the North West Wilts District. The troop consisted of 30 boys but the search was on for more members and a Scoutmaster.

1   Chamberlain, J.A., (1976)
2   *Wiltshire Times*, 29 October 1932

The site was acquired on 'favourable terms' with Sir Audley Neeld and was gifted by an anonymous donor. The cost of £500 for the build had already been helped by £220 of donations and fundraising by the scouts themselves.

Troop committee member Walter Rudman drew up plans for free.

The building, which still stands today, was made with a wooden frame with expanding steel and stuccoed cement outside. The interior was panelled with oak on the bottom half and creamed coloured walls on the top half. The space inside was suitable for up to 70 scouts and could comfortably seat 200.

The contract was awarded to Messrs Blackford & Sons of Calne. Mr Blackford gave the flagpole as a gift.

1st Chippenham Boy Scouts mark their 21st Anniversary, at their Audley Road headquarters in 1932. Postcard - Paula Champion.

At the opening ceremony, there were 140 scouts from all over North Wiltshire, along with Chippenham Cubs with Cubmaster Robinson. The Scouts were inspected in the road opposite by the mayor and local Scout officials. Once the mayor had turned the key in the door the hall was declared open. A tea was held inside with a sing song and reminiscences of the early days of Chippenham Troop shared by Jeff Dyke.[1]

1 *North Wilts Herald*, 1 November 1929

For five years during the Second World War period, the hall was used as a 'British' Restaurant. It was handed back at an official ceremony in July 1946. The hall is still used by the Scouts to this day.

27th October 1902

All schools in Chippenham were ordered to close from this date for two months, due to an outbreak of measles, scarletina and diphtheria.

Several cases of scarletina ended with fatalities. Within the next few weeks, John and Caroline Hart of 61 Parliament Street lost two children. On 3 November, Ada Maud, their eldest daughter age eight. On 6 November, Gertrude Annie, their youngest daughter age one year and eight months. Then tragically a third the following month on 2 December, Herbert William, their son age three years and ten months.

Their loss was handled poorly, with debates over who was responsible. The Reverend Bardwell tried to divert blame on the parents citing a lack of co-operation with the council. This was vehemently denied by the father who claimed two of the three children were denied admission at the hospital due to overcrowding.[1] However the parents acted, the insensitive behaviour of some of those in 'authority' was certainly uncalled for.

28th October 1931

In High Street, a large crowd had gathered outside the town hall to wait for the general election result and police were on the scene to ensure traffic could pass through the town. Alfred George Duke from London, who was caught up in the excitement, waved at an acquaintance as he drove through and steered erratically, knocking down one of the constables. Fortunately he was not hurt and Duke apologised there and then, and because of this and his admission of guilt and regret when he later appeared in court, he was let off, only having to pay £1 costs.[2]

The Chippenham election result was a Conservative hold for Victor Cazalet.

---

1   *Bath Chronicle*, 6 November 1902.
2   *North Wilts Herald*, 13 November 1931.

29th October 1924

On this day, Captain Victor Cazalet was first elected as MP for Chippenham at the General Election. His victory was secured with a majority of 2212 over the incumbent Liberal MP Mr Alfred James Bonwick.

Probably one of the most notable MPs in the history of the constituency, Cazalet was an important figure on the international scene. He tragically died, after 19 years an MP for Chippenham, in a plane crash at Gibraltar in 1943.

The Cazalet memorial in Bath Abbey. Peter and Olympia Cazalet were great grandparents to notable Chippenham MP Victor Cazalet.

The Cazalet family was prominent and wealthy, with many connections to high society. Queen Victoria was a frequent visitor to their south of France residence and was godmother to Victor, who himself was godfather to the actress Elizabeth Taylor. There is a memorial to his great grandparents in Bath Abbey.

30th October 1868

At about 10.45pm an earthquake was 'distinctly felt' in Chippenham. Many reported being woken by their beds being rocked. Those still awake could hear the ground shake along with the windows, doors and shutters of their homes. A poorly little girl at Rowden Hill told her nurse that someone had been shaking her bed![1]

In a letter to the Meteorological Magazine, Mr Fermor Bonnycastle Gritton, resident of West Tytherton, returned his own account. This included an aftershock at around 3am the following morning. His daughter jumped out of bed thinking the house was 'about to fall'. Some inhabitants of small cottages only a quarter of a mile away were so

---

1   4 November 1868, *Frome Times*.

shaken that they sat up the rest of the night in fear.[1]

There was a belt of activity spreading northeast from Exeter to Nottingham. 'Many were greatly alarmed' including Anne Little, wife of a porter Jesse Little at the station. All the furniture and windows began to rattle in her home at Rowden Hill Cottages. Mr Cooper's canary behaved in a 'most extraordinary manner' but was calm as soon as the shaking had stopped. Mr Thomas, junior, felt 'a cold shudder pass completely through him' and the chair he was sat on 'oscillated three times from west to east'.

The recorded epicentre of the magnitude 4.9 earthquake was at Neath, near Port Talbot, Wales.

31st October 2007

Wiltshire & Swindon History Centre opened on Cocklebury Road. The previous accommodation for the county archive, was called the Wiltshire and Swindon Record Office and was situated in a former mattress factory in Trowbridge. This building at Bythesea Road, was declared sub-standard by the National Archives in 1998. Despite this, a move to Chippenham wasn't universally popular, but the new centre has proved its worth since opening.

Cowlins started construction on 28 June 2005, with the foundations, superstructure and roof all in place by 6 December 2005. The cost was £11.1 million, met without Lottery funding as the council's bid was rejected. 30,000 boxes of archival material were moved before opening.[2]

NOVEMBER

1st November 1993

Work began to dismantle the old Buttercross, which stood in the Castle Combe Manor House kitchen garden behind where Castle Combe Primary School used to be. It was moved to storage in a stonemason's yard for safekeeping whilst permission was finalised for the repositioning in the market place.

1 *The Meteorological Magazine*, Volumes 3-4.
2 www.wshc.eu

A few days later, a small celebration took place, at which Mayor James Gore received a symbolic single roof tile for safekeeping.[1]

The Buttercross was originally part of the Shambles and was positioned where the closed Barclays Bank stands today. It was used as a buttery and later for the sale of meat. It had stood in the garden at Castle Combe since 1889, when it was sold for £6 to the manor house for use as a gazebo. It was first visited by the Civic Society in 1984 for inspection. The stone columns needed repairing and a new roof frame as a scale drawing from the 19th century showed the correct length was 8m not 7m as it had been reassembled in Castle Combe. The Society bought it for £300. This money was used to repair the Castle Combe bridge.

2nd November 1987

The Olympiad Leisure Centre held its topping out ceremony. This is an 'ancient Scandinavian custom' of planting a spruce tree on the top of a building during its construction, to 'ward off evil spirits'. It was later removed and planted safely in the park. Wimpy Construction director Lewis Toman and Chairman of North Wiltshire District Council David

The footbridge was slowly moved to position on 22 August 1987. Photograph - Chris Toombs.

1   *Civic Society Bulletin*, issue 67, November 1993.

Hartley toasted with a pint of beer, an ancient English custom!

A second ceremony also took place in connection with the new leisure centre, on this day. The footbridge which crosses the river between Island Park and the Olympiad was officially opened. Pupils from Monkton Park and Ivy Lane Schools were the first to cross the bridge and the Sea Cadets fired a gun from a boat underneath. Kirsty Hearn from Monkton Park School and Amanda Jenkins from Ivy Lane School, both age 10, read from 'scrolls of friendship' to the headteachers of their opposite school. Kate Barrett of Yewstock Crescent cut the ribbon, and a commemorative plaque was unveiled by Councillor Hartley in the centre of the bridge.

Sadly, within a year the bridge had been vandalised and had to be closed off for five days whilst fixed, the side rails having been kicked out. Whilst there, they also took the chance to improve the decking, as small gaps were causing problems for those wearing high heels![1]

3rd November 1863

The Calne Branch line opened to passenger traffic for the first time.

This was a much bigger, public event, than that on 29 October when the first ever train arrived in Calne at 8:30am. It was loaded with 100 pigs for John and Henry Harris' pork processing factory.

The 3 November was an unofficial holiday in Calne. An estimated 1000 passengers travelled on the train in one day, while many more were left behind in the heavy rain due to lack of space.[2]

A ticket for Calne to Chippenham from 1955.

4th November 1779

St Nicholas Church was consecrated by Robert, Bishop of London. The church was built in a classical Georgian style from plans drawn up by the architect John Wood 'the Younger', who is best known for The Royal Crescent and The Circus in Bath. Now Grade II listed, it was built from Box Stone, replacing an earlier church which was demolished around

1 Gazette? 1988.
2 Tanner, p.7.

Hardenhuish Church. The Ricardo monument can be seen to the right.

1778 and that stood 200 metres downhill opposite Hardenhuish Rectory. Many of the internal features predate the existing church, so may have been transferred at this time. The entire works were paid for by Joseph Colborne.

5th November 1915

The Red Cross Hospital at the Neeld Hall received their first convoy of troops. Ten wounded soldiers were transferred to Chippenham from Southmead Hospital in Bristol after only a few weeks back in England.

This plaque on the front of the town hall is currently the only visible memorial to the Red Cross Hospital.

Of the new patients, one was from the Western Front but the other nine were evacuated from Gallipoli. Only one came by stretcher with the rest being walking-wounded. Local businesses did their bit to help the Ambulance Corps to transport the men from the station. Chippenham Laundry Company lent a van and Burridge's Motors a car.[1]

---

1   *Wiltshire Times,* 13 November 1915.

6th November 1954

A large crowd were attracted to the town hall hoping to catch a glimpse of Gwen Berryman, better known as Doris Archer from the BBC Radio programme 'The Archers'. Miss Berryman was there to open the Congregational Church's Autumn Sale. She was once a teacher in a Congregationalist Sunday School, so it was a cause close to her own heart. To give thanks, Jennifer Catt of the Greenway Lane Congregational Sunday School, presented her with a bouquet.[1]

7th November 1956

The seizure of the Suez Canal was condemned by Jim Callaghan, at a protest meeting in Chippenham. Callaghan was MP for Cardiff East at the time, but would later become leader of the Labour Party and Prime Minister. He argued that Sir Anthony Eden had deliberately launched the country into war making 'Britain's honour damaged'. A Conservative element was able to infiltrate the audience and began to heckle Callaghan. Britain was also losing support of the Commonwealth because of its actions and its oil supply was under threat, according to Callaghan, who argued for a change in government. Robert Portus, the prospective Labour candidate for Chippenham also spoke, arguing that the country was being led into a Third World War.[2]

Chippenham Cottage Hospital, London Road.

8th November 1897

The foundation stone of the cottage hospital was laid by Lady Dickson-Poynder, whose husband Sir John Dickson-Poynder, was the first to put forward the idea of establishing one as a permanent commemoration of Queen Victoria's Diamond Jubilee. The hospital opened on London Road in January 1899.[3]

1 *Wiltshire Times*, 13 November 1954.
2 *Wiltshire Times*, 9 November 1956.
3 *Bath Chronicle*, 19 January 1899.

9th November 1943

Farmer Alfred Bridgeman, aged 73, was killed when an RAF Mosquito crashed into Rawlings Farm at Cocklebury. Both the pilot, F/Sgt Leonard George Mayhew and navigator, Sgt Leonard Edward Cable, were also killed.[1] Witnesses saw how the aircraft was already on fire as it ploughed through the cowshed and stable, before colliding into the back of the farmhouse. Mrs Bridgeman was rescued by two young members of the farm staff, Avice Dickinson and Harold Whitmarsh. Mr Edwin Albert Self of Cocklebury Farm ran to the nearest telephone to summon the fire brigade. A bucket chain was formed to throw water on the fire but the water pipe was fractured. A considerable amount of time passed before the NFS and the RAF could start pumping a sufficient supply from the river, over half a mile away.[2]

Mr Bridgeman was trapped in the house. Rescuers desperately tried to reach him as he cried for help for half an hour, but when they did it was too late.[3]

10th November 1914

The first official group of Belgian refugees arrived in Chippenham.

After a public meeting, it was agreed that the offer of help should be made to the Belgians. Five families totalling 20 people were 'received as guests of Chippenham', and provided with lodgings at the Bath Brewery Company's old West End Club, rent free.[4]

The committee for providing accommodation for the Belgian Refugees included the Mayor, Lady Muriel Coventry and Aldermen Coles and Neale. They arranged the 'fitting up' of the old West End Club as a home and the appeal for furniture had yielded a good response from the townsfolk.

Several families of refugees had already been provided for by 'private enterprise' but the West End Club initiative was to be the Town's response.[5] On 15 October 1914, an earlier, unofficial group of Belgian refugees, arrived and stayed at Mr Richmond's former home in Union Road.[6]

1 chippenham1939-1945.weebly.com
2 *Wiltshire Times*, 13 November 1943.
3 *Gloucestershire Echo*, 10 November 1943.
4 *Western Daily Press*, 13 November 1914.
5 *Wiltshire Times*, 31 October 1914
6 *Wiltshire Times*, 14 October 1939.

West End, Park Lane. Accommodation was made available here for Belgian refugees in 1914.

Many of the leading townsmen offered to pay a subscription of 10 shillings a week, which was the estimated minimum cost to keep one of the families. Others chose to pay lump sums of £10-£20.[1]

11th November 1918

The news that the Armistice had been signed reached Chippenham just before 11 am. Upon hearing this, everyone in the town stopped working and the rest of the day was set aside for 'general rejoicing' of an impromptu character.' Soon there were flags flying, church bells ringing and cheering crowds in the streets. What started as a cloudy morning turned into a day of continuous rain, but this didn't stop the revellers. A procession of munition workers, with the 'munitionettes' along with other factory workers, was led by the Salvation Army band through the town to the market place. There, it ended with singing of the 'Doxology' and a meeting presided by Alderman Townsend. Thanksgiving services were held at the churches, and after speeches were made in the market place, another procession took place.

1   *Wiltshire Times*, 31 October 1914.

12th November 1903

A parish church choir concert was held at St Andrew's National School in St Mary Street. Performances included those by Miss Nell Hill, violin soloist and Thomas Augustus Trotman, flute soloist. Mr Jacob sang 'Abide with me' and Mr Dyer was a whistling soloist. A comedy was also staged; 'The Blind Beggars' by Rev Thomas Geoffrey Henslow and Justly William Awdry.

There was a crowded audience which led to financial success for the event.[1]

Thomas Trotman was well known in Chippenham for his professional photography. Originally from Croydon, he was new to the town and by 1911 he was living at 'Highfield' in Lowden Avenue.[2] Much of the photographic record we have of Chippenham from this period, is thanks to his work.

13th November 1822

Four horses were brought to the door of the White Hart in preparation for the arrival of the 'White Lion Coach'. But, when they were left alone for a moment, they quickly set off towards Bath Road.

Close to the Chippenham toll bar, a boy managed to stop one of the horses long enough to mount it and he chased after the others but he had no success in stopping them. The horse collided with a wagon in Batheaston, injuring its shoulder, but fortunately not hurting the boy. One of the other horses was stopped in Grosvenor Place. The other two finally came to a stop of their own accord, at the White Lion in Bath, their intended destination.[3]

14th November 1936

At 2pm, the opening of the Gaumont Cinema in Timber Street took place with Mayor George Lane Culverwell officiating. Harry Falls was presented with an illuminated address, and a cheque, which had been subscribed to by 110 people. This was a magnificent token of appreciation for the previous ten years he had served as manager of

---

1 *Wiltshire Times*, 14 November 1903.
2 1911 census.
3 *Bristol Mercury*, 18 November 1822.

the old Palace Cinema, and for his work in bringing the Gaumont to Chippenham, where he continued as manager there. The new cinema had capacity for 1100 patrons, a massive boost to the town's entertainment facilities.[1]

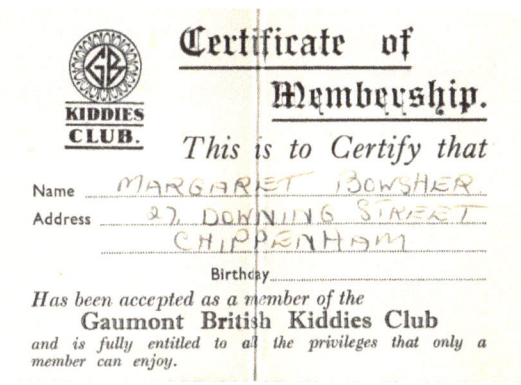

Gaumont British Kiddies Club membership card. Paula Champion.

15th November 1952

Three premises in the town were broken into by Harold Gordon Fricker of London. During his crime spree, he stole; four suitcases from George Mattingly's (51 Market Place), silverware worth £1,164 from Henry Stanley Dickenson's

Numbers 51-52 Market Place is currently occupied by Julian House charity shop and number 53 is Coiffure hair salon.

1   *Wiltshire Times*, 14 November 1936.

(53) and then gold bars, foil and £3 from William Alfred James, Dental Surgeon (52).

To enable this series of thefts, part of a wall was removed to get into Dickenson's and from there Fricker could access Mattingly's next door and James' upstairs.[1]

16th November 1928

A 'hurricane' made its way over south-west and central England. At Spye Park, Captain Anthony Napier Fane Spicer, aged 37, was struck by a falling tree, whilst he went for a walk. The spot at which he was found is called Egypt Hill. He died instantly, crushed by the trunk of the tree. The Beaufort Hunt was cancelled that week as a mark of respect. Spicer was buried at nearby Chittoe Church.

Damage to local property included; part of the goods shed roof blown off at the railway station, and the top eighteen feet of a sixty foot chimney belonging to Messrs Downing & Rudman, that was demolished by the power of the wind. The 14 men working in the sawmills below it, all miraculously escaped unharmed.[2]

17th November 1922

A pig dealer from Kington Langley was discovered to be breaking Swine Fever regulations. Louis Lenoerts claimed to be transporting pigs from Somerford to Melksham when stopped by police, but they were later found in Chippenham market.

Police Constable Griffen asked Lenoerts why he had made a wrong statement, but Lenoerts believed he could do as he wished as long as his register was kept up to date. Superintendent Wells argued at court that this was a lie. Lenoerts had been in similar trouble before so the court had little sympathy fining him £10 for his infringements.[3]

18th November 1944

In September, Chippenham Town's black opponents were barred from entering the Co-operative Hall (now Salvation Army) in Foghamshire

---

1   *Wiltshire Times*, 10 January 1953.
2   *Somerset Standard*, 23 November 1928.
3   *Wiltshire Times*, 23 December 1922.

Hardenhuish Park off Bristol Road. Home to Chippenham Town Football Club.

after the match, for an event ran by a Swindon dance band.[1] The doorman who refused the men entry, claimed he was merely enforcing the colour bar to stop black and white service personnel from mixing, as requested by the US Army. There had been a division of American soldiers camped at Hardenhuish.[2]

One witness commented that 'it looks as though the Americans are being allowed to rule England'. An RAF serviceman who had accompanied the Jamaicans said - 'its a bad show when these boys, who are British Empire subjects, give up their afternoon to entertain Chippenham people and then are snubbed in this way'.[3] As such, 'strong indignation was aroused' amongst the football community of the town. To show it was not the Chippenham way, the club invited the RAF team, who comprised mainly of Jamaican born pilots, back for a return match.

Afterwards, the two teams sat together for tea at the British Restaurant and then later for a social supper at a local club. Photographs of the men together were taken and kept by both teams.[4] Club Secretary Fred Evans said they were 'the nicest lot of chaps anyone could wish to meet'.[5]

1 *Evening Advertiser* 20 September 1944.
2 *Daily Mirror*, 21 September 1944.
3 Davis, J., (2015).
4 *Daily Mirror*, 20 November 1944.
5 *Daily Mirror*, 21 September 1944.

'Harlem Renaissance' writer Eric Walrond, who had lived in Bradford on Avon for some years after leaving the States, wrote of Chippenham; 'the heart of the town was unquestionably sound' and had 'put paid to the colour bar'.[1]

'Mr T Bunker, a member of the district committee of the Amalgamated Engineering Union, said the trade union movement in the town felt very strongly about this matter and would take steps to establish the principle that there should be no colour bar in Chippenham. He said the AEU and the Electrical Trades Union would be passing resolutions of protest at their next meeting, and would also bring the matter before the Chippenham and District Trades Council.'[2]

19th November 1883

Suspicions had been raised that one of the parishioners of St Paul's was taking from the collection. The suspect was Mary Pearce, who had been staying behind to clean the church. Inspector Collett planted a florin, two shillings, two sixpences and a French penny. Later, he saw Richard Pearce, Mary's nephew, leave and go to a pub for a pint of beer. Collett found that he had used the florin, so arrested him. He then went back into St Paul's and made Mary turn out her pockets, where he found the other coins and the key to the collection box. Upon checking the box, he found it was empty apart from the French Penny.[3]

On the 1881 census, the Pearce family lived at Parry's Yard off St Mary's Street. Richard was an 'apprentice ginger beer maker', possibly in Dicky Fry's factory at the Three Cups in the Shambles.

20th November 1987

Norris McWhirter presented trophies and prizes at Chippenham Technical College's awards evening. He was best known as a TV personality and for his work with the Guinness Book of Records. He lived nearby at Kington Langley.[4]

1 Davis, J., (2015).
2 *Evening Advertiser* 20 September 1944
3 *Bristol Mercury*, 20 November 1883.
4 *Wiltshire Times*, 27 November 1987.

21st November 1880

A boy named George Stroud departed Horatio Nelson Minty's farm at Thingley, to deliver milk to the Condensed Milk Factory, when he came across a man frozen to death, led across the road. The poor man was James Hall, landlord of the Harp & Crown at Gastard near Corsham. Hall had been into Chippenham the day before to see about his licence. On the way home he stopped first at the Rowden Arms for a pint of ale and then at the New Inn (now The Pheasant) for more, leaving there at around six.

From the marks on his body and examination of his surroundings, it appeared that he dropped his umbrella in a ditch. He then struggled in and out of the ditch to retrieve it and, soaked through, he froze and collapsed on the road.[1]

James Hall was aged 62 when he died and was buried in Corsham on 25 November 1880. He left behind a widow, Lucy Hall.

22nd November 1752

St Cecilia's Day was chosen as the date to unveil the new church organ at St Andrew's. A 'grand performance by very eminent hands' was

St Andrew's Church as it was in 1813.

1   *Taunton Courier*, 24 November 1880

given during a service at 11am, and in the evening there was a Ladies Ball. Tickets were sold at the White Hart (now Iceland supermarket) and the Angel Inn in the market place, for 2s 6d each. In the mid 18th century this was equivalent to about £15, or a days wages for a skilled tradesmen.[1]

The easternmost bay in the more modern north aisle, is occupied by the organ and its superb eighteenth century case. Arguably the most outstanding treasure in the church, it was built by Bruce Seede of Bristol that year, although was twice restored in 1879 and then much more sympathetically in 1965.

23rd November 1993

Fog caused a 22-car pile up on M4 motorway near Chippenham. Six people were injured and two police cars were damaged by vehicles which failed to stop.[2]

24th November 1841

Jonathan Dale and Henry Prestnell broke into Elizabeth Hull's shop in Christian Malford and stole several items of drapery. They gained access by removing the glass from the window during the night. Stolen items included forty pairs of stockings, in excess of forty handkerchiefs, some waistcoats and yards of printed material. Guilt was confirmed when £20 worth of these were found in their possession. At Devizes Assizes on 20 July 1842, they were sentenced to ten years transportation.

Henry Prestnell, age 21, was sent to 'Van Diemen's Land' (Tasmania) on the 'Moffatt' along with 388 other male convicts, on 10 August 1842, arriving at Hobart on 28 November 1842. So far it has not been possible to locate a record of whether Jonathan Dale, age 28, was also transported.

25th November 1906

The Mayor received a letter from Sir Dighton Probyn, the Keeper of the Privy Purse, including a postal order for £3 on behalf of his Majesty the King, as a donation to Mrs Davis of Timber Street who had

---

1   *Salisbury & Winchester Journal*, 6 November 1752.
2   *Guardian*, 24 November 1993.

given birth to triplets.[1] This payment was known as the 'King's Bounty'.

Thomas and Mary Davis christened the children Noah (after Thomas' father), Thomas and Elisha. They were described as 'strong children' with 'every appearance of living'.[2] Thomas was a hawker of fish and fruit. Mary was the daughter of William Wood who had a shop on the Causeway, also in the fruit sales business. At the time of the birth, the family had grown to five children all under the age of 2 years and 4 months old.[3]

26th November 1968

It was the official opening of the multi-purpose Bridge Centre Youth and Welfare Complex. It had already been in use since July.

This new facility's success depended on 'the youth, elderly and handicapped' helping each other, according to Wiltshire County Council Chairman Sir Henry Langton. Mayor Arthur Evans also took this view, asking for adult volunteers to help run the centre.[4]

Staff were employed in May for the July opening. Young people from the existing youth centre in Lowden Avenue helped to make it ready.

The recently completed new town bridge and weir did little to prevent flooding caused by a huge downpour and a foot of water filled the Bridge Centre. The canoe club based at the centre offered lifts through the waters.

When the roundabout was created around the centre, workmen thought they had hit a water pipe when a jet shot into the air creating a giant fountain. It turned out to be one of the many springs in this part of town.

It stood in the middle of the one way system on Bath Road and was originally built as a Territorial Army Centre in 1958 at a cost of £73,000. After only eight years, the building became redundant in 1966 and it was nearly used for another purpose. The North Wilts Water Board were interested in moving there from their home in Marshfield Road (now the Whale & Dolphin Charity), which they had been seeking to extend, and move to the old drill hall to centralise their facilities including using part as living accommodation for control room staff.[5]

1   *The Salisbury Times*, 7 December 1906.
2   *Newbury Weekly News*, 6 December 1906.
3   *Wiltshire Times*, 29 December 1906.
4   *Gazette & Herald*, 28 November 1968.
5   *Wiltshire Times*, 9 December 1966.

The building was demolished in 2016 and the space is now covered in wildflowers during warmer months.

27th November 1901

Opening of Sheldon Road Primitive Methodist Church. The church cost £1200 to build. An extension was completed in 1989 at a cost of £140,000.

The first Primitive Methodist Chapel was replaced by Sheldon Road Methodist in 1901. It survived as part of Chequers Yard until 2019 when it was demolished for new houses.

The Methodists first established at Lowden in 1855 with the chapel and Sunday school at what became Chequers Yard. In comparison, this much simpler structure was built using land gifted by John Silas Banks Dowding and 5000 bricks given by Mr Rixson, at a cost of £120. This chapel was demolished in 2019 to make way for 1-4 Chequers Yard.

28th November 1956

A freak storm struck Chippenham just before noon. For half an hour, hail and snow fell heavily causing visibility to be almost non existent. Several inches settled and driving conditions were severe. Then,

Sheldon Road Methodist Church has stood on the corner of Sheldon Road and Audley Road since 1901.

in an equally unexpected manner, once it stopped the sun began to shine and the snow melted almost as quickly as it had arrived.[1]

29th November 2014

After nearly twenty years of campaigning, work finally began on making Chippenham Station accessible for all. As part of a £3 million access scheme, the 115 year old footbridge which spanned the tracks, was taken down and replaced with a new structure with lifts to the platforms. This was due to be completed in the following spring but delays meant that it wasn't complete until 22 January 2016. These were caused by unexpected utility cables discovered in the dated infrastructure needing to be identified and diverted.

Further work would still be required to enable step free access from the Hathaway Retail Park side of the tracks.

The successful campaign was the work of former Chippenham mayor and councillor Maureen Lloyd who led the Community Access to Rail

1   *Wiltshire Times,* 30 November 1956.

Travel group (CART) from November 2007. They fought for equal rights for the disabled, especially those in wheelchairs, who previously had to book ahead to be escorted cross the tracks.

30th November 1911

Miss Natalia Janotha, court pianist to Kaiser Wilhelm II of Germany, visited the town hall. She was a Polish pianist and composer who studied under many well known composers including Brahms. She performed for the courts of Prussia, England and for the rulers of Spain and Italy until being appointed court pianist in Berlin in 1885. Later, she lived in London, but in 1916 was deported under suspicion of being an enemy alien. Unusually, Janotha would insist on having her dog on stage, within her view, during all her recitals. In 1905, she made four recordings, including one of Chopin's unpublished 'Fugue in A minor'; she owned the manuscript of his work. She also wrote several books about Chopin, aided by her personal connections with his family.

At Miss Gwendoline Teagle's concert in the town hall at 8pm on Thursday, evening every seat was filled, various lords and ladies were present as well as the mayor. Miss Teagle sung and Miss Janotha, 'whose manipulation of the intricacies of Chopin will not be easily forgotten,' was on the piano.[1]

DECEMBER

1st December 1816

The town mill was burnt to the ground in an apparent act of arson. A few days earlier, an anonymous threatening letter addressed to Francis Head, clothier, was found under his front door.[2] The author threatened to set fire to the mill if Harry Goldney the bailiff didn't inspect the weights and measures being used in the town.

The mill was the property of Thomas Edridge and occupied by Messrs Gaby and Dowling. Although destroyed by the fire, it was quickly rebuilt.

1 *Wiltshire Times*, 2 DEcember 1911
2 *Bulletins of State Intelligence.*

The town mill was demolished in 1957 as part of a modernisation plan which included a new row of shops and eventually a new town bridge.

A date stone of '1817' has been discovered and is now in Chippenham Museum.[1]

Date stone salvaged from the town mill when it was demolished in 1957. It was rediscovered in Goughs Solicitors, who donated it to Chippenham Museum in 2015.

2nd December 1869

The Chippenham Literary & Scientific Institute was inaugurated by its first elected president, Mr Goldney. The aim was for inhabitants from all classes and political persuasions to meet for 'mutual recreation and mutual instruction'.

There was standing room only in the Neeld Hall, where a variety of interesting objects and scientific instruments were placed on tables, along with refreshments laid on by Mr Goldney. He then gave a lengthy speech about his hopes and aims for the Institute and shared stories of interest, including his recent visit to

Sign from the Literary Institute in the Market Place. Chippenham Museum Collection.

1   Chamberlain, p.138

Weymouth with Sir Daniel Gooch, where he was shown around Brunel's SS Great Eastern, which was later used to lay under sea telegraph cables.[1] Replacement paddle-wheels for the SS Great Eastern were made at Brotherhood's factory in Chippenham in 1862.

3rd December 1909

Suffragettes visited Chippenham. A large crowd attended a meeting of the National Women's Social and Political Union, at the Temperance Hall. The purpose was to explain their 'militant tactics up to date'. The hall was full well before the start time of 7.30 and many were left disappointed to not get in.

A suffrage demonstration in Chippenham, c1910. Chippenham Museum Collection.

It soon became clear that the majority did not want to allow the talk to take place. The two ladies who took to the stage were greeted with 'ironical cheering' and the blowing of a horn. Miss Rachel Barrett attempts to raise her voice above the crowd were completely futile and the reporters were unable to take comments. After ten minutes, Miss Marie Naylor tried but was met with an equal level of noise.

William John Ainsworth of Swindon and the Rev Henry Bayley Bardwell then got to the stage to try and speak but soon retreated

1 *Devizes and Wiltshire Gazette*, 9 December 1869.

as well. Miss Naylor then got back on to the stage and continued to speak for half an hour to a barrage of noise and rowdy behaviour. The two ladies then quietly slipped away. The police were present, led by Superintendent Moore, but they did not need to get involved.[1]

Marie Naylor was staying at the Suffragette's Retreat called Eagle House in Batheaston where many prominent WSPU members passed through. She took part in the Pantechnicon Raid on 11 February 1908 when a large group of suffragettes used two large furniture delivery vans as 'Trojan Horses' to attack Parliament.

Rachel Barrett was joint organiser of the WSPU campaign after Christabel Pankhurst fled to Paris in 1907 and was also Editor of *The Suffragette* magazine.

William John Ainsworth was a councillor in Swindon and former manager of the Wilts & Berks Canal. His daughter Kathleen Ainsworth was a suffragette. By 1913 she was secretary of the Swindon & North Wilts branch of the National Union of Women's Suffrage Societies.

Rev Bardwell was a Baptist minister and Liberal who lived at Orwell House, Chippenham in 1911.

4th December 1925

Francis Daly of Abergavenny, along with George Money and Arthur Hawkins of no fixed address, were charged with breaking into a branch of the Co-operative Society on Sheldon Road (now OneStop). They were also charged with stealing petrol from a garage in Sutton Benger.

At 2.15 in the morning, Daly was leaning over the bonnet of a Morris-Cowley two-seater in Audley Road. He was spotted by PC Webb, who asked him what he was doing, to which the reply was that he had lost his way in the fog. After receiving directions for Bath, Daly drove off but in the wrong direction. PC Webb then went round to the back of the shop and heard noises inside. On closer inspection he found that a window had been smashed. As Money came towards the door, PC Webb was able to handcuff him, but Hawkins managed to escape out the front and got into Daly's car which had returned. Both men were picked up later in Marlborough. Hawkins admitted the offence but claimed his motive was hunger. Daly admitted to aiding his escape.

1   *North Wilts Herald*, 10 December 1909.

OneStop at Lowden was built in 1922 as a Co-operative Society store.

Francis John Horton, manager of the Co-op, confirmed that the only item stolen was some citron peel.[1]

5th December 1931

It was the Salvation Army Jubilee, celebrating 50 years of the corps in Chippenham. A reunion tea was held with Colonel Fitzgerald in attendance. Also present were Bandmaster Frank Tinson, a product of the Young People's Corps and his father, George Tinson, still playing the bass euphonium at the age of 82.

The Salvation Army had received rough treatment when first coming to Chippenham. In the summer of 1881, three officers visited and arranged the first meeting, helped by local sympathisers. However, their open-air events were met by much opposition. Their banners were targeted, rubbish was thrown at members and there was even one attempt to throw their leader, Captain Sutton, in the river.

Other churches already established in the town either showed no interest in this mistreatment or even preached against the Salvation Army movement.

Mr Bardwell provided a new meeting place in one of the arches of the

1   *North Wilts Herald*, 18 December 1925.

The Salvation Army Citadel.

viaduct, and gradually conditions improved for the Army in Chippenham and a band was formed in 1884. They moved to Bath Road in the early 1890s where the Citadel was built in 1903, but later moved to the former Co-operative Hall in Foghamshire (April 1971) where they are still residing today.[1]

6th December 1927

Henry John Rudman and Israel Webb were both summoned to court charged with moving an unmarked pig in a Foot and Mouth Disease infected area. The pig was licensed but also was required to be marked. Webb, on Rudman's instruction, was taking the animal by horse and cart to be slaughtered. Rudman claimed the pig was for his own consumption and had never been in trouble throughout his 35 years keeping pigs. Both men claimed to have been ignorant of the rules, but still received a 2s 6d fine.[2]

1 *Wiltshire Times*, 12 December 1931.
2 *North Wilts Herald*, 6 January 1928.

7th December 2001

It was a big day for Chippenham, as Queen Elizabeth and Prince Philip arrived for their rescheduled visit. It was originally planned for March but was delayed due to the Foot and Mouth crisis.

Their train pulled into Chippenham Station at 10.58. The Queen and Prince Philip were met by a crowd of hundreds waving Union Flags and various dignitaries including Mayor Barbie Dawson.

The Queen walks with Mayor Barbara Dawson and Mace-bearer John Wade along the High Street. Photograph by Tony White - Chippenham Museum Collection.

Prince Philip visited Wiltshire College just after 11am, meeting with students to discuss their work. He then visited Abbeyfield School, which he officially opened with the unveiling of a plaque. Afterwards he was off to the town centre to unveil another plaque. This time it was to launch the second phase of the creation of Chippenham Museum's new home. The first floor galleries and education room were due to be completed in June 2002. Then he met the Queen, after a short walk to the high street for the town hall.

8th December 1954

A dinner was held in honour of Alderman Herbert 'Bert' Cruse, who retired from the position of works manager of Westinghouse Brake

& Signals after 18 years. He had served a total of 52 years as an employee of the company. Cruse didn't leave completely though, as he stayed on as a director.

Joining Westinghouse as an office boy in 1902, the highlight of his career was probably receiving a CBE from the Queen at Buckingham Palace, for 'public and industrial services'. He also welcomed Queen Mary at the works in April 1944, when she visited to view the armament production taking place.

Cruse was also active in local politics and was the only man to have been elected as a peacetime Mayor of Chippenham three times in a row.[1]

9th December 1839

The Duchess of Cambridge, Prince George and Lord Chesterfield passed through the town in the afternoon, on their way to visit the Duke of Beaufort at Badminton. The Duke of Cambridge was also expected, but he went to Badminton by another route.

A large crowd had gathered by the White Hart Inn, and as the seven carriages of the royal party passed, bells were rung and the people cheered.

Prince George, the only son of the Duke and Duchess, was 20 years old at this point. He would go on to marry an actress named Sarah Fairbrother in 1847, a union which was unrecognised by law as it contravened the Royal Marriages Act. His cousin Queen Victoria simply pretended that Sarah didn't exist.[2]

10th December 1937

Scoutmaster Edwin Hane arranged the 1st Chippenham Boy Scouts annual 'bun fight' at the Scout Hall. This event included an 'excellent tea' and parlour games. Each of the Scouts were able to bring a non-Scout friend to show them the benefits of joining. This proved effective as a number did sign up at the event.[3]

A 'bun fight' is another name for a type of party, usually one where lots of people are expected. There is no fighting involved (usually!) but often there is a scramble for food, hence 'bun fight'.

1   *Wiltshire Times*, 11 December 1954.
2   *Wiltshire Independent*, 12 December 1839.
3   *North Wilts Herald*, 17 December 1937.

11th December 2011

After a six hour clean up, volunteers from Calne Divers removed three lorry loads of rubbish from the river near the town bridge. More than 40 trolleys, 20 bicycles and a 1980s bus stop with bin and timetable still attached, were hauled from the depths. Other interesting items included traffic cones, pushchairs, car wheels, a cash register, numerous road signs, a cash machine sign, a bollard, a pack of newspapers, a stereo system and hundreds of bottles and glasses. The age of the items suggested that it had been at least 30 years since a clean up had been done, if ever.

The plan was to clear a half-mile stretch between the bridge and the footbridge by the golf course at Monkton Park, but only 25 metres were completed after a days work. The water was thick with silt, meaning the divers had to feel their way around underwater. Five of the ten divers became ill later, with Weil's disease being suspected.

Mayor David Powell and his wife spent several hours, literally getting their hands dirty, by helping to pull everything out of the water.

12th December 1966

The Order of the Yugoslav Flag was presented to Chippenham's Bernard Woods and fellow potholers of the South Wales Caving Club, by Mr. Sarakcic, the Yugoslav Ambassador, on behalf of President Tito.

They had been invited to explore the Balinka Pit, a 1,000ft.-deep cave about 60 miles south-west of Zagreb, in the hope they would find the bodies of four Yugoslav partisans. They were successful in finding the remains of the men who had been wartime comrades of Tito himself.

The communist partisans organised the wartime resistance in Croatia against the Germans and were later declared national heroes. On 2 April 1942, they were murdered by guerrillas known as the Chetniks and their bodies were thrown down the vertical pot-hole.[12]

13th December 1902

An elopement caused considerable excitement in the town on this day. Nelson Rose, a driver employed at the Angel Hotel by Richard

1   *The Times*, 13 December 1966.
2   www.gowerhiddenhistory.blogspot.com

The Angel Hotel, c1909. This became the premier coaching inn after the closure of the White Hart, which was blamed on the popularity of the railway.

Careless, who was married with seven children, had left the town. At the same time, a married woman who was associated with Rose, disappeared as well.

Mr Careless reported missing money, to the sum of £3 1s, to the police who then began an investigation. The pair were traced from Trowbridge, where they had a pram in their possession, to Bristol, by a record of boxes being sent ahead of them in Rose's name. They ended up in Newport where they had taken lodgings under the pretence of being a married couple. A Sergeant Waters of the local police, tracked them down and arrested Rose for embezzlement and brought him back to Chippenham by train. By now the news of the affair had spread like wildfire and a large crowd of curious townsfolk had congregated at the station.[1]

On the 1901 Census, Rose can be found living at 105 Wood Lane with his wife Annie and their seven children.

14th December 1830

The son of Rawleigh and Ann Eddolls of Hardenhuish, died after falling into a boiler of boiling wort.[2] Wort is beer at the unfermented stage of its production. Robert Eddolls, was only 3 years 4 months old

---

1   *Somerset Standard*, 19 December 1902.
2   *Bristol Mercury*, 21 December 1830.

when the accident happened.[1]

15th December 1867

An attack by a group or Irishmen, described as Fenians, took place in the town. Several inhabitants were injured, with one being left for dead. Police quickly arrived to take control of the situation, making two arrests. This came two days after Britain's first terrorist bombing, the Clerkenwell Outrage, an explosion in London which killed twelve and injured 120. It was organised by the Irish Republican Brotherhood in a failed attempt to breakout two Fenian prisoners.

16th December 1981

Nine year old Sarah Tuck of Marshall Street, received the 'Children of Courage' award at Westminster Abbey from Princess Michael of Kent. Afterwards she met with celebrities Morecambe and Wise and Adam Ant at an honorary lunch in the House of Lords.

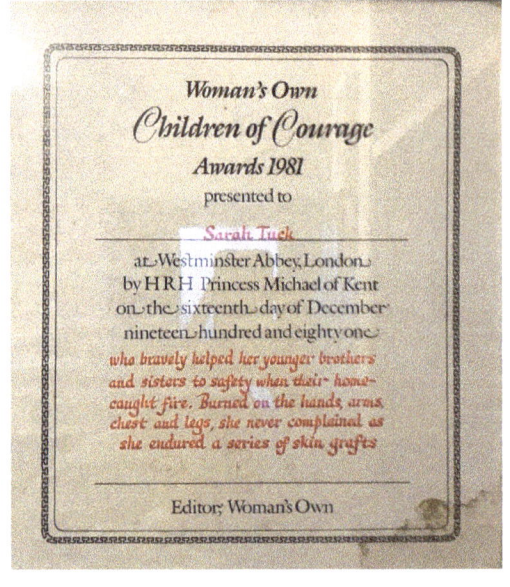

Sarah saw flames spreading up the stairs of her old home in Yatton Keynell and bravely guided her four younger brothers and sisters to the bathroom where their father was able to lower them from the window, down to Martin, her 11 year old brother. She was was burnt in several places but didn't notice until she was in a neighbour's house afterwards.

17th December 1937

Burtons Tailors shop opened on this day at 1-3a Market Place on the corner of River Street. The foundation stones on each front facing corner of the building, bear an inscription similar to those found on all

1   *Wiltshire Times,* 18 December 1937.

The foundation stones laid by three of Montague Burton's children.

Burtons shops of the era. They are marked with the names of Montague Burton's three children.

An advertisement that appeared in a local newspaper, hailed the architecture as 'a living monument to the quality, integrity and economy of its services.' A group of London contractors were brought in to build rather than any local firms. This was because Burtons had a certain pattern and style that they wished to replicate across the country.

In 2020, Arcadia, who owned Burtons, went into administration. The shift towards online retail, coupled with the effects of the coronavirus pandemic, were to blame. In February 2021, thousands of jobs were lost. These included Dorothy Perkins who were also part of the Arcadia group, and had a shop in Emery Gate from when it opened in 1986.[1]

18th December 1926

Through the raising of voluntary contributions, a wireless was purchased and installed at the Poor Law Institution at Rowden Hill, otherwise known as the Workhouse. The wireless was the idea of Mr Pierce, the master.

A ceremony was performed by the mayor in front of Guardians, subscribers and 'inmates'. Later, a greeting came through from the London radio station welcoming the Chippenham Poor Law Institution to the list of wireless subscribers.[2]

19th December 1966

The first subway was opened in Chippenham. This was part of the new inner-relief road layout around the Western Arches at Marshfield Road and New Road. When it opened, work was still ongoing and

1   *Wiltshire Times*, 18 December 1937.
2   *Wiltshire Times*, 25 December 1926.

pedestrian safety was a concern. Two more sections of subway still needed to be built. The subway went under Marshfield Road and it was intended that pedestrians would be diverted to use this route, effectively bypassing many of the shops.

Traders in lower New Road were not happy, as this effectively diverted all footfall away from their shops. To counter this issue, the council agreed to open a temporary footpath for use until the work was completed.

It only took a few weeks for graffiti to start appearing. To improve the appearance of the subways, local schools took part in a Civic Society scheme which included murals reflecting the history of the town.

20th December 1922

The Neeld Hall was the venue for a Cottage Hospital Prize Draw. Before the carnival, events like this would be used to raise vital funds. The collection of prizes was arranged by Louis Brown who was well known as an 'indefatigable worker'. The draw was a great success as Brown sold 7,446 tickets with the help of his friends.

Butter churns were borrowed from Hathaway's for prize numbers and tickets. Two nurses were in charge of shaking the churns and Brown selected the tickets. A fine selection of prizes were won.[1]

21st December 1839

Elizabeth Clifford, a young women described as having 'weak intellects', escaped from the Union Workhouse, which at that time was at The Butts. A leaflet campaign was used to seek news of her whereabouts, but sadly her body was later found in the river near Chippenham Mills.

Clifford had previously been a servant in the employ of Rev Robert Ashe, then Rev John Matthews, both at Langley Burrell, before taking ill. At the workhouse she only spoke once in weeks, saying she would be 'in the river before Christmas'. The workhouse master had been concerned for her health and had applied for her to go to a lunatic asylum but this was prevented due to costs.[2]

---

1 *North Wilts Herald*, 22 December 1922.
2 *Wiltshire Independent*, 7 February 1839.

The M4 motorway under construction in the 1960s. Photograph - Jackie Harding.

22nd December 1971

The M4 Motorway was completed after opening in sections, of which four did so in 1971. Motorists could finally carry on past Junction 15 at Swindon for a further 50 miles to join the rest of the route to London at Holyport interchange near Maidenhead.

There the official tape cutting ceremony took place, with junior minister Michael Heseltine, Parliamentary Under-Secretary of State for the Department of the Environment, doing the honours. He was the first to drive the whole 140 miles, of which he dubbed the 'New Welsh Way', delivering a message from the Lord Mayor of London to the Lord Mayor of Cardiff. Once the ceremony had concluded, invited guests were taken by coach to Stanton St Quintin. Leigh Delamare Services were still under construction nearby and opened in 1972.

Original designs for the motorway included a route south of Chippenham or another north of it but very close to Castle Combe!

23rd December 2015

Barber Alan Shepherd retired after nearly 40 years cutting hair. From 1977 to 2003, Alan had kept a shop in Fleet Road, close to John Coles Park. The shop was previously owned by George Whitehead, who also lived in the house adjoining it. Unusually for a barbers, Alan used an appointment only service.[1] In 2003, Alan sold his shop and went mobile, so he could carry on serving his regulars.[2]

Alan Shepherd standing outside his barber shop in Fleet Road, mid 1990s, prior to him taking part in the London Marathon. Photograph - Alan Shepherd.

24th December 1905

There was a burglary at the workhouse on Christmas Eve. Albert Charles Jones (alias Forbes) broke in and stole £20 worth of jewellery, belonging to the workhouse master's brother-in-law who was visiting from London.

Later whilst Jones was imprisoned in Edinburgh for another theft, he made a statement admitting a list of similar crimes and gave information to the police which helped them recover nearly all the stolen jewellery. He had disposed of the missing pieces on Durdham Downs at Clifton, Bristol.[3]

1 *Gazette & Herald*, 9 December 2002.
2 *Gazette & Herald*, 1 December 2015.
3 *Bath Chronicle*, 22 March 1906.

Albert was convicted of burglary at Salisbury Assizes on 6th June 1906 and sentenced to five years penal servitude, which he spent at Dartmoor prison.

25th December 1990

In the first couple of minutes of the Christmas morning service at Kington St Michael, storm winds toppled the south east pinnacle of the church tower, sending it falling forty feet and landing on the roof of the nave. Roof timbers prevented much of the stone from falling, but a 'large piece of masonry, a number of broken timbers and a mass of Cotswold stone tiles' fell into church. This happened during the first hymn 'In the Bleak Mid-winter'. The Churchwarden's pew was demolished but luckily he was still attending to latecomers at the door.[1]

St Michael & All Angels Church, Kington St Michael, May 2022.

Four parishioners were taken to Chippenham Hospital by ambulance to receive treatment, one of whom had been knocked unconscious.

1 visionwebsites.co.uk/Uploads/Site126/Files/churchtowerrepairs.doc

Other significant damage in the area included at Sheldon Manor, where a 60ft, 500-year-old yew tree was blown over just missing the 13th century porch.[1]

26th December 1924

Joseph Henry Buckle, fishmonger and captain of the Chippenham Fire Brigade, married Minnie Doris Johnson on Boxing Day, in what was described as a 'unique ceremony'.

The event 'aroused widespread public interest' due to the fact that not only was Joseph one of the most respected tradesmen in the town, but also because it had been assumed he had 'received on a life of confirmed bachelorhood'.

It was a fireman's wedding and they came from several towns, all in uniform including the bridegroom himself. The Trowbridge brigade arrived on their motor fire pump which was 'gaily decorated' with white ribbon. They collected Buckle from his house in the high street and he stood on the engine for the journey.

An archway of axes from the church door to the pavement was created by the firemen. The rain disappeared just before the happy couple came out and a rainbow appeared from behind the church. This was regarded as a good omen by many in the large crowd, who were watching in the market place. The couple were then whisked away by Chippenham Brigade's own motor fire pump, along with several relatives.

On route to the Angel Hotel, they stopped at the cenotaph where Minnie laid her bouquet, whilst Joseph saluted. After their reception, they left for their honeymoon in London.[2]

This day was also Joseph's birthday. He was born at the Bear Hotel on this date in 1873. His mother had only just been made a widow, his father dying on 22nd November aged just 44 years old.

27th December 2008

The fastest red card in the history of football (at the time) was awarded to David Pratt of Chippenham Town FC during their fixture with Bashley FC. Pratt was sent off three seconds into the game for lunging at Bashley's Chris Knowles.

1   *Wiltshire Times & News*, 28 December 1990.
2   *Wiltshire Times & Trowbridge Advertiser*, 3 January 1925.

The previous record was held by Giuseppe Lorenzo of Italian club Bologna. He was dismissed after ten seconds in 1990 when he hit a Parma player.[1]

28th-29th December 1903

The original Little George Inn was destroyed by a fire on this night. The Turner family who lived and worked in the pub, were rescued thanks to the quick actions of Lieutenant Thomas Hathaway, of Chippenham Fire Brigade. A stable lad, Herbert 'Bertie' Banks aged 18, lost his life despite the best efforts of Thomas to save him.

Public subscription paid for the funeral and headstone of Bertie Banks who died in the fire at the Little George in 1903.

Mary Turner, the Landlady, was woken by the smell of the fire and managed to rouse her husband. The staircase was alight so they had to escape through a window. The origin of the fire was never discovered.

One of those who heard the cries for help was Hathaway who was working late at his father's premises. He got a ladder and with the help of others managed to get Arthur Turner and his wife, Miss Parker, the barmaid and Miss Haines, a servant, out of the window and to safety.

He then climbed to the roof of the building himself to search for the stable lad and called to him with no response. Then Hathaway, entered the building to try and rescue Banks.

The flames were too great, and no success was made in fighting them due to poor water pressure. Eventually, after two hours, the fire was brought under control, but only the lower half of the building was saved.

A parrot and a cat were found dead, suffocated by smoke. A dog escaped with the Turners.

1   *Guardian*, 29 December 2008.

Entry into the remains was only possible after 10 hours, which was when the stable lad was found by the back door.

At the time, Mr Turner was the Secretary of Chippenham Town Football Club and was looking after the books, players kit and the 'second-class' tournament cup, but these were all lost to the fire.

Hardenhuish Brook can quickly rise after a period of heavy rainfall.

Banks' parents lived in River Lane, St Mary Street (Common Slip).[1]

An inquest into the death of the 18 year old, was held at the Temperance Hall. Mr Turner believed that the fire started in a cupboard next to the fireplace where rubbish was stored.

Banks was found resting on his elbow and it was clear to the jury that he died of suffocation. The inquest urged that the coroner should make contact with the town council about the inadequate water supply for that part of town. They also commended Lieutenant Hathaway and Mr Turner for their attempts to save the boy's life.[2]

A collection was held by the patrons of the pub to help pay for the young lad's burial and this can be found close to the cemetery entrance on London Road.

30th December 1859

An 'extraordinary hailstorm' occurred in Chippenham, along with 'vivid flashes of lightning and loud claps of thunder'. The sheer volume of rainwater caused many roads to become impassable. Hardenhuish Brook rose causing a number of the 'poor labourers cottages' to be flooded. Many homes close to the River Avon suffered the same fate.[3]

This was a prelude to what was described as a 'hurricane' or 'tornado' which first hit land at Bowood and ploughed through North Wiltshire and became known as 'The Great Storm of 1859'. It was the worst seen in Wiltshire for many years.

31st December 1899

When William Light's carpentry shop and timber yard in Union Road was destroyed by fire in July 1897, he never recovered from the shock and his health rapidly declined.[4] He had a 'slight attack of influenza' which gradually worsened and he died at his home in New Road at 4.30 in the afternoon, age 72 years of age. Many important contracts were carried out by his company including church restorations.[5] Light was an active member of the town council and mayor

1 *Wiltshire Times*, 2 January 1904.
2 *Bath Chronicle*, 7 January 1904.
3 *Devizes and Wiltshire Gazette*, 5 January 1860.
4 *Wiltshire Times*, 24 January 1931.
5 *Bath Chronicle*, 4 January 1900.

A Light & Co bill head used before the merger with FW Hulbert & Co.

in 1895.[1] A Conservative and member of the Constitutional Club, he was also deacon of the Congregational Chapel and had only recently retired from office of superintendent of the sunday school.[2]

After his death, his son carried on the business as 'W V Light & Son'. This merged with F W Hulbert & Co in the 1930s, becoming 'Hulbert, Light & Co.[3]

1   *Bristol Mercury*, 2 January 1900.
2   *Wiltshire County Advertiser*, 6 January 1900.
3   Chippenham Civic Society, Grand Designs; Builders and Buildings of Chippenham.

ACKNOWLEDGEMENTS

Below is a list of people who have helped in some way with my research for this book.

Ray Alder, Bakers of Nailsea, Melissa Barnett, Julie Baskerville, Simon Bensley, Nick Burridge, Cassandra Campbell, Paula Champion, Ron Challinor, Chippenham Museum, Melissa Dallimore, Elaine Davies, Julie Davies, Shane Davis, Tamsin Delahaye, Chris Dunster, Di & Mike Eaton, Dave Edwards, Deborah Etherington, Adrian Full, Tim Gatherum, David Gearing, Tom Geddes, Jackie Harding, Emma Hildebrandt, George & Doreen Howell, Peter Jefferies, Marian Jones, Sarah Lane, Trisha Lewis, Don Little, James Lutener, Linda Martin, Jean Morrison, Roger Palmer, Nick Powell, Janice Robinson, John Scragg, Nick Selby, Claire Selman, Alan Shepherd, Michael Slater, Caroline Smith, Chris Southall, Steve Spear, Dave Stone, Julie Townsend, Tony White, Lucy Whitfield.

BIBLIOGRAPHY

Alder, R., (2011), *Chippenham and the Wilts & Berks Canal*, Hobnob Press.
Behe, G., (2012), *On Board RMS Titanic: Memories of the Maiden Voyage*, The History Press.
Bowen, C., (1969), Flying Saucer Review, Sept/Oct 1969, Vol.15, No.5.
Buss, G., (2004) *Great is Thy Faithfulness: 200 Years of God's Goodness at Chippenham*, Olive Press Ltd.
Callow, Henry, (1989), The History of the Chippenham to Calne Road Walk.
Chamberlain, Joseph A., (1976), *Chippenham: Some Notes on its History*, Chippenham Charter Trustees, Chippenham.
Coggles, J. & N., (1998), *The History of St Mary's Parish, Chippenham, 1855-1998*, St Mary's Roman Catholic Church.
Cook, A.A., (1906), *Asser's Life of King Alfred*, Ginn & Company.
Daniell, J.J., (1894), *The History of Chippenham*, Houlston.
Davis, J., (2015), Eric Walrond: A Life in the Harlem Renaissance and the Transatlantic Caribbean.
Davis, Julie., (2016), *From Blackout to Bungalows: WWII Home Front Wiltshire and the Austerity Years 1939-1955*, Hobnob Press.
Endacott, F.J., (1978), *Westmead Junior School, Chippenham 1858-1978: A Brief*

History, Unknown publisher.
Goldney, F.H., (1889), *Records of Chippenham relating to the Borough, from 1554 to 1889*, Unknown publisher.
Harper, C.G., (1899), *The Exeter Road*, Chapman & HallHarting, J.E., (1891), The Zoologist.
Henson, B., (1982), *Pew Hill House, Chippenham: A Brief History*.
Horton, B., (1995), *West Country Weather Book*
Kilvert's Diary
MacLachlan, Tony, The Civil War in Wiltshire Meaden, G.T., (1984), 'Shower of Tadpoles...,' Journal of Meteorology.
Penny, John, (1999), *Up, Up and Away!*, Bristol Branch of the Historical Association.
Platts, Arnold, (1947), *A History of Chippenham - AD 853-1946*, Wiltshire Gazette, Devizes.
Tanner, G., (1972), *The Calne Branch*, Oxford Publishing Company.
Taylor, K.S., (2012), *Dry Shod to Chippenham: A History of Maud Heath's Ancient Causeway*, Ex-Libris Press.
Twydell, D., (1986), *Defunct F.C*, Unknown publisher.
Wilson, A. & M., (1991), *Chippenham & Lacock in Old Photographs*, Alan Sutton Publishing.

Other Sources
The British Medical Journal, 16 October 1869.
Bulletins of State Intelligence Re Town Mill 1817.
Causeway Methodist Church Diamond Jubilee Year, souvenir handbook, 1956.
General Post Office notice, 4 February 1782.
Hansard, Commons Sitting, 1 July 1964.
Hansard, 30 July 1998.
The Industrial Railway Record, issue 24, April 1969, pp44-47.
The Lifeboat, Journal of the RNLI, November 1927.
The Meteorological Magazine, Volumes 3-4.
Parliamentary Papers, volume 20, 1894, pp132-133.
Primitive Methodist Magazine, October 1855.
The Wiltshire Archaeological & Natural History Magazine, vol 25-26. 48

Websites
chippenham1939-1945.weebly.comnarpo-wilts.org.uk
www.pglwilts.org.uk/lodges/north-wiltshire/lansdowne-lodge-of-unity
www.christianbookshops.org.uk
www.soroptimistinternational.org/about-us/historychippenham-twinning.org.uk/la-fleche
www.bbc.co.uk/news/uk-england-wiltshirefreebmd.org.uk
www.visionwebsites.co.uk

www.wshc.euwww.diyweek.net
www.gowerhiddenhistory.blogspot.com
chippenham-twinning.org.uk/la-fleche
cinematreasures.orgpro-patria.co.uk
www.motorsportmemorial.org
www.historicracing.com
motorwayservices.uk/History:Leigh_Delamere
www.jsf.hiddentigerbooks.co.uk
www.kingtonstmichael.com

From Ancestry.co.uk
Australian Convict Records Index, 1787-1867.
England, Andrews Newspaper Index Cards, 1790-1976.
England & Wales Criminal Register, 1791-1892, Wiltshire 1823.
WWII, Index to Allied Airmen Roll of Honour, 1939-45.
UK Census Collection

Chippenham Civic Society
Bulletin issues; 64, 67, 68, 69, 75, 94, 95, 98, 99, 127, 142, 143, 149
From website - Grand Designs; Builders and Buildings of Chippenham.
Chippenham *Civic Society Bulletin*, Sheldon School Celebrates Half Century, article by Caroline Fowke.

Newspapers Aberdeen Press & Journal, *Bath Chronicle*, *Belfast Telegraph*, Birmingham Daily Post, *Bristol Mercury*, The Cambrian News & Merionethshire Standard, *Chippenham News*, Civil & Military Gazette (Lahore), Coventry Evening Telegraph, *Daily Herald*, *Daily Mirror*, *Devizes and Wiltshire Gazette*, The Era, Evening Express, Frome Times, *Gazette & Herald*, Glasgow Courier, Gloucester Journal, *Gloucestershire Echo*, *Guardian*, Hampshire Advertiser, Kentish Weekly Post, Leeds Mercury, Lloyd's Weekly, Los Angeles Times, Morning Post, *Newbury Weekly News*, *North Wilts Herald*, Northern Echo, The Pall Mall Gazette, The Police Gazette, Reading Evening Post, Reynolds' Newspaper, Rhos Herald, Rhyl Record & Advertiser, *Salisbury & Winchester Journal*, *Salisbury Times*, Shepton Mallett Journal, Somerset *Guardian* & Radstock Observer, *Somerset Standard*, The Sun (London), Sunday Mirror, *Swindon Advertiser*, Taunton Courier, *The Times*, Warminster & Westbury Journal, Weekly Mail, *Western Daily Press*, Western Mail, Western Times, *Wilts & Gloucestershire Standard*, *Wiltshire County Advertiser*, *Wiltshire Independent*, *Wiltshire Times*.

Wiltshire & Swindon History Centre
F8/180/27 - Englands Social Centre, Chippenham (1946-1955)
G19/154/19 - Instructions for Police Officers and Watchmen, Chippenham

Borough Council, Agreements, (1832).

1769/83 - Pamphlet recording the work of 25 years of Chippenham Borough Council 1889-1914 by E. Newall Tuck. Includes a brief list of street improvements and a longer list of public works. (1916).

J1/105/9 - Carnival Committee Minutes. (1933-1938).

G19/996/3 - Miscellaneous ephemera (20th c).

F14/424/45 - Flood prevention scheme, River Avon, at Chippenham Town Centre. (1960-1962)

INDEX

Abbeyfield School 28, 68, 208
Acton Turville 141
Adams, Albert Edward 73, 74, 82, 164
Adlam, Thomas Henry 166
Ainsworth, William John 204, 205
Allied Shoes 122
Amalgamated Society of Railway Servants 144
Ambulance Training Centre 62, 102
Ancient Order of Foresters 9
Andrews, Anita 21
Andrews, Giles Bullock 38
Anglo-Swiss Condensed Milk Factory 9, 10
Archard, Reginald George 88
Archard, Wilfred 158
Army Cadets 91
Arthur's Well 39, 40, 110
Ashe, Chris 76
Ashe, Rev. Robert 214
Asser, John 5
Atyeo, John 87
Attrill, Frank 81
Aubrey, John 1
Audley Road 105, 113, 159, 181, 182, 201, 205
Austin, Alderman 9
Austin, Charles Edward 38
Austin, Mrs 38
Avenue La Flèche 152, 153, 159
Avon (the hamlet of) 89
Awdry, Daniel 77, 88
Awdry, Edmund Mainley 38, 74
Awdry, Edmund Portman 133

Bacon Factory 31, 36
Back Avon Bridge 66, 140, 150, 155, 181
Bailey, Charles 34, 35, 55, 56
Bakehouse, The 42
Baker, Charles 36
Baker, Joan 93
Baker, Mrs 59, 140
Baker, Oliver 59

Baker, Reginald 134
Baldwin, Stanley 95
Bamjee, Dinshaw Sorab 42, 43
Bank House 10, 39, 110
Banks, Herbert 'Bertie' 79, 219
Banks, John 79
Banks, John Silas 200
Baptist Chapel 48, 94
Barrett, Henry 11
Barrett, Joshua 120
Barrett, Kate 187
Barrett, Police Superintendent 180
Barrett, Rachel 204, 205
Bath Coach, The 40
Bath Hospital 40, 168
Bath, Marquis of 42
Bath Road 39, 67, 68, 69, 71, 82, 110, 128, 129, 150, 158, 170, 192, 199, 207
Barclays Bank 186
Bardwell, Rev. Henry Bayley 142, 144, 183, 204, 205, 206
Barley Close 5
Barnard, James Frederick 93
Baydons Lane 36, 127
Baylis, Percy 61
Baynton, Sir Edward 29
Beaufort, Duke of 139, 141, 148, 209
Beale, Joan Stopford 109
Beard, Alfred 69
Beazer Projects Ltd 123
Becher, Sir William 87
Belcher, Francis William 139
Belgian refugees 190, 191
Bendry, Edward 121
Benn, Anthony Wedgwood 106
Bensley, George William 52, 53
Bernard, John 24
Berryman, Gwen 189
Biddestone 89, 97, 109, 129, 131
Billett, George Francis 102
Billington's Super-Save 122
Bingo Hall 83, 84, 112

Black Bridge, The 102, 157
Blackford's Ironmongers 118
Blunsdon, Albert John 38
Boer War 125
Bonallack, Nigel 86
Borough Lands 6, 26, 106,
Borough Parade 128
Borough Surveyor 73, 82, 91
Boville 132
Bowerbank, Marion 115
Bowles, William Lisle 29
Bowood 28, 118, 119, 130, 221
Bowd, Janet 39
Bowd, Leslie 39
Boyes, Arthur 134
Bradford on Avon 33, 196
Bradley & Sons 173
Bradley, John Henry 109
Brassey, Colonel Hugh 165
Bray, Sidney 121
Bridge Centre, The 113, 199
Bridgeman, Alfred 190
Brinkworth, Robert Edwin 169
Brinkworth, William Henry 9
Briscoe, Dr William Thomas 136
Bristol Road 4, 67, 68, 69, 73, 84, 146, 195
British Restaurant 183, 195
Britten, Frank 134
Britton, John 1
Brockbank, Sgt John Thomas 32
Broderstad, Astrid 45
Bronson, Bruce 45
Bronson, Gilbert 45
Brook Ground 58
Brooke Bond Oxo Factory 79, 80, 83
Brooks, Robert 134
Brotherhood's Railway Works 48, 204
Brown, Louis 214
Bryan, Thomas 10
Bryant, George Rourke 165
Bryant, William 150
Bryant, William George 61
Bubbles 4
Buckle, Joseph Henry 'Joe' 56, 82, 137, 172, 218
Bullock, Mr 41
Bulson, Eric 5
Bulwark Transport 54, 55

Burge, Judith 93
Burger, Dr Franz 133
Burgess, Mr 91
Burgesses 27, 72
Burghley, Lord 102
Burn's Day Storm 16, 17
Burridge, William Millman Brown 93
Burtons 27, 28, 212, 213
Busby, Geoffrey 81
Butler, Charles 110
Butler, Herbert 38
Butler, John 69
Butt, Robert 10
Buttercross, The 46, 99, 185, 186
Butts, The 98, 214

Calne 14, 15, 16, 24, 29, 39, 52, 72, 98, 117, 120, 124, 152, 156, 157, 182, 187, 210
Careless, Richard 15, 211
Castle Combe 38, 71, 117, 168, 185, 186, 216
Cazalet, Victor 183, 184
Chippenham Cottage Hospital 9, 11, 19, 79, 97, 131, 144, 189, 214
Chippenham Fire Brigade 14, 16, 19, 56, 82, 91, 108, 139, 180, 190, 218, 219
Chippenham Laundry 164, 188
Chippenham Literary & Scientific Institute 74, 203
Chippenham Museum 11, 28, 32, 45, 50, 59, 71, 83, 96, 97, 99, 104, 107, 118, 130, 137, 156, 179, 180, 203, 204, 208
Chippenham Railway Station 4, 13, 21, 29, 61, 119, 141, 155, 169, 173, 175, 194
Chippenham River Festival 142, 143
Chippenham Sea Cadets 53, 81, 91, 140, 187
Chippenham Soroptimist Club 43, 44
Chippenham Swimming Club 2, 56, 133
Chippenham Town Football Club 75, 147, 195, 220
Chippenham United Football Club 70, 106
Church;
 Causeway Methodist 178
 Central Methodist 145
 Congregational 189, 222
 Lowden Methodist Chapel 200

    Monkton Hill Methodist 145
    Sheldon Road Methodist 200, 201
    St Andrew's 6, 17, 50, 85, 118, 168,
      171, 172, 197
    St Mary's 38,
    St Paul's 34, 118
    St Peter's 135, 136, 176, 177
    Wesleyan 158
Church, John 7
Cinemas;
    Astoria 83, 84
    Gaumont 28, 45, 81, 121, 192, 193
    Palace 11, 12, 13, 193
Clifford, Elizabeth 214
Clutterbuck, Mr 16
Clutterbuck, Edmund Henry 130
Cocklebury 4, 53, 59, 61, 75, 190
Cocklebury Lane 174
Cocklebury Road 47, 61, 75, 81, 138, 168,
    169, 185
Coles, John 9, 47, 48, 169, 179, 190
Collier, Violet 30, 31
Common Slip 222
Constitutional Club 39, 53, 222
Cook, Derek 127
Cook, Ethel Dorothy
Cook, Frederick 30, 165
Cook Street 55
Co-operative Society 13, 27, 57, 113, 114,
    115, 121, 181, 194, 205, 206, 207
Cork, The Earl of 15
Cowley, Colin 14
Cox, Deborah 164
Cox, Police Sergeant 27
Crew, Tony 28
Culverwell, George Lane 91, 105, 192

Dale, Jonathan 198
Daly, Francis 205
Dallas Road 31, 180
Daniell, Rev John Jeremiah 149
Dank's Down Cottage 117
Davies, Maureen 93
Davis, Elisha 199
Davis, Mary 199
Davis, Noah 199
Davis, Ted 86
Davis, Thomas 199

Davison, Thomas Henry 63
Davison, Mary Elizabeth 63
Dawson, Barbie 208
Day, Henry 134
Dear, George 91, 107
Deeker, Joseph 66
Dentons Ironmongers 103
Derriads Farm 67
Derry Hill 29, 75, 103, 106, 161
Devizes 58, 70, 81, 99, 105, 132, 133, 140,
    142, 152
Devizes Assizes 198
Dickenson, Henry Stanley 193, 194
Dickinson, Avice 190
Dickson, Miss 149
Dickson-Poynder, Sir John 9, 130, 169,
    189
Dickson-Poynder, Lady 168, 189
Disasters;
    Fire 10, 14, 16, 18, 19, 26, 55, 79, 82,
      83, 139, 140, 149, 154, 158, 177, 178,
      190, 202, 219, 220, 221
    Flood 1, 2, 13, 51, 71, 72, 89, 108, 111,
      112, 113, 123, 155, 156, 180, 181,
      199, 221
    Sinkhole 54
    Spanish Flu 14, 170
Dixons 122
Doggett, Leonard 14
Dorothy Perkins 122, 213
Dowding, Francis Edward 9
Downer, Cyril 121
Downing & Rudman, Messrs 74, 115, 194
Downing Rudman & Bent, Messrs 126,
    127
Downing Street 39, 40, 78, 91, 92, 93
Dowett, Cornet 132
Dowett, Major Francis 132
Dryden, Ronald Maura 168
Dyer, Mr 192
Dyke, Henry 69
Dyke, Jeff 182

Eastern Avenue 123
Eaton, Joseph William 141
Eddolls, Ann 211
Eddolls, Rawleigh 211
Eddolls, Robert 211

Emery Gate Shopping Centre 93, 122, 213
Emery Lane 93, 94, 95
Enforde, John 108
Englands 26, 32, 104, 138
Escott, Reginald 158
Evans & O'Donnell 49, 120
Evans, Trevor 32
Extreme weather;
    Fog 174, 198, 205
    Gale 11, 12, 13, 18, 146
    Hail 200
    Heat 115
    Hurricane 11, 17, 194, 221
    Lightning 78, 89, 119, 154, 221
    Snow 41, 51, 200, 201
    Thunderstorm 71, 78, 221
    Waterspout 81
    Wind 17, 18, 19, 66, 194
Eyles, Alfred George 36

Factory Lane 30, 36, 78, 82, 147, 148, 165
Falls, Harry 192
Farmer, Arthur 147
Farnewell, Henry 72
Fellowes, Mr 41
Ferfoot 23, 24
Ferris, William 89
Fields, Frank 98, 158
Finkenagel, Mary 63
Firlands 68
Firs, The 70, 106
Fisherton Gaol 23
Fitzgerald, Colonel 206
Fleet Road 216
Flower, Benjamin 70, 71
Flower Show 126, 130, 146
Flying Dutchman, The 57
Flynn, Maurice 127
Foghamshire 15, 16, 19, 51, 54, 56, 65, 111, 113, 132, 150, 180, 181, 194, 207
Folk Festival 7, 86, 87
Folly, The 68
Ford 117, 143
Fortune, William 75
Foundry Lane 49, 61, 126
Fox, Charles 66
Fox, Harriet 66
Fox, Joseph Stanley Victor 66

Fox, Sidney Herbert 66
Fraher, Patrick 127
Frank's Grocery Shop 18
Freemasons 56
Freer, Dawn 76
Fricker, Harold Gordon 193, 194
Frogwell 18, 45, 167
Fry, Dicky 196
Fuller, David Gordon 168
Furey, Dr Joseph William 136

Gainey, John 110
Gale, William 69
Gardner, Harry 150
Garrett, Mrs 106
Gartland, Rosemary 123
Gartland, Tom 123
Gastons Road 159
Gasworks 44
General Post Office 20
Gerick, Herman 25
Gibbons, Kathleen 97
Gibbs, John 20
Gibbs, Mary 176
Giddeahall 109
Gingell, Joan 115
Gladstone Liberal Club 161, 162
Glen, Walter 126
Goldiggers 45
Golding, Bert 59
Goldney, Ann 82
Goldney, Frederick Hastings 38
Goldney, Harry 202
Goldney, Sir Gabriel 113
Goldney, Sir John 158
Goldney, Sir Prior 50
Golf Club 74, 123, 210
Gore, James 186
Gough, Sidney Ivor 40
Grant, Dave 173
Great Bustard 24, 25
Great Western Railway 15, 53, 57, 65, 82, 89, 141, 155, 174, 175
Greenhalgh, Frank 111
Greenway Farm 181
Greenway Gardens 18
Greenways Maternity Unit 44, 45, 90
Gregory, Gerald H 14

Gregory, William 97
Griffen, Police Constable 194
Griffith, Jonathan 179
Grittleton House 130, 146
Gritton, Fermat Bonnycastle 184
Guardians, Board of 52, 213
Gurney, William Henry 140
Guthrum 5
Gutter Lane 94

Haines, Miss 219
Hale's Bakery 51
Hall, George 27
Hall, James 197
Hall, Lucy 197
Hall, Thomas 180
Hamlet, The 81, 102
Hampton, Frederick William 44
Hampton, Henry 44
Hancock, Florence 36, 165
Harris, Eric 83
Hart, Ada Maud
Hart, Caroline 183
Hart, Gertrude Annie
Hart, Henry Albert 166
Hart, Herbert William 183
Hart, John 183
Hart, Louisa 55
Hathaway, Michael James 70
Hathaway, Thomas 219
Hardenhuish Brook 111, 220, 221
Hardenhuish Lane 159
Hardenhuish Manor 16, 17, 33
Hardenhuish Park 5, 47, 77, 87, 95, 130, 195
Hardenhuish Rectory 188
Hardenhuish School 14, 109, 159, 167
Hartley, David 187
Hawkins, Arthur 205
Hawkins, Grace 176
Hazell, Elizabeth 117
Hearn, Kirsty 187
Heath, Malcom 26
Hedges, Reginald 30, 31
Helme, Colonel Sir George 9, 74
Henslow, Rev Thomas Geoffrey 192
Hetherington, John 181
Hibberd, Edgar Nelson 127, 128

Hibberd, James 9
Hibberd, William 128
High Street 1, 13, 18, 27, 58, 78, 85, 86, 93, 94, 108, 111, 115, 116, 118, 119, 121, 137, 149, 150, 154, 180, 181, 183, 208, 218
Hillier, Ann 117
Hillier, John 117
Hodges, Sergeant Leonard 174
Holland, Miss 'Bobs' 173
Holloway, Henry 4
Holloway, Thomas 55
Holly, Ethel 158
Holly, Kathleen 158
Holly, Mrs 158
Home Ground 58
Horse & Flower Show 126
Horton, Francis John 206
Howell, Reginald 147, 148
Hulbert, Heather 93
Hulbert, Light & Co 222
Hull, Arthur 57
Hull, Joseph 150
Hull, Frank 38
Humphreys, William Francis 156
Humphries, Isaac 69
Hungerdown Lane 70, 121, 177
Hunt, John Victor 42
Hygrade 8, 83

Irwin, Hughie 76
Isaac, James 150
Island Park 110, 187
Isolation Hospital 30
It's a Knockout! 76
Ivy Fields 87, 163, 164
Ivy Lane 6, 56, 68
Ivy, The 74, 150, 170, 179, 181

Jackson, Rev John Edward 34, 41, 42
Jacob, Mr 192
James, William Alfred 194
Janotha, Miss Natalia 202
Jay, Dr Henry Mason 9
Jefferies, Ernest John 28
Jeffries, Les 76
Jennings Amusement Fair 98
Jennings, Dick 146

Johnson, Minnie Doris 218
Jones, Albert Charles 216
Jones, Daniel 33
Jones, John 181
Jones, Rev William 178
Joyce, John 124
Jubilee Institute 101, 146
Juvenile Court 42, 100

Keary, Alfred John 171
Keary, William 172
Kellaways 24, 42, 43, 50
Kelson, Charles 151
Kelson, Mary Ann 151
Kelson, William James 151
Kemp, Phoebe 84
Keene, William 101
Kilmartin, Evelyn 93
Kilvert, Francis 89, 150, 172
King & Son, William Charles 16
King Alfred the Great 5
King Alfred Street 134
King Edward VII 118
King George III 26
King George VI 77, 78
King Henry VIII 29
King William IV 151
King, Cecil 67
King, Mr 36
King's Bounty 199
King's Street 108
Kingston, Mrs 79
King, Tom 143
Kington Langley 4, 37, 39, 57, 112, 149, 194, 196
Kington St Michael 1, 217
Kinnier, Arthur Charles 38
Kirby, John 136
Knight, Henry 150
Knight, Janet 39
Knight, John 58
Kopp, Joseph Theodore 11

Labour Hall 61
Labour Party 61, 106, 189
Lacock 4, 25, 26, 38, 69, 86, 89, 132, 181
Lacock Abbey 164
Lacock Halt 175

Ladyfield Brook 111
Ladyfield Housing Estate 106
Ladyfield Road 97, 102, 111, 112
Lair, George 110
Lambert, Thomas Herbert 38
Landsend 11, 49
Langley Burrell 33, 34, 64, 120, 214
Langley Green 24
Langley Road 112, 181
Langley Signal Box 173
Langley, Victor 158
Lansbury, Angela 61
Lansbury, George 61
Lansdowne Lodge 56
Larkham Rise 50
Laverton, Winifred 23
League of Friends 45
Leigh Delamere 34, 41, 146, 215
Lenoerts, Louis 194
Lenton, William George 114, 164
Lewis, Joseph 101
Liberal Party 47, 57, 75, 113, 144, 161, 162, 184, 205
Light, William 221, 222
Lineen, Anne 50
Little, Anne 185
Little, Jesse 185
Lloyd, Geoffrey 109
Lloyd, Maureen 202
London Road 7, 9, 18, 20, 45, 50, 53, 67, 68, 79, 84, 96, 101, 115, 132, 134, 172, 189
London Road Cemetery 99, 126, 127, 151, 170, 221
Long Close 2, 53, 133
Long, Robert 76
Long, Sir James 132
Lords Lane 116, 139
Lords Mead 135, 136
Lovell, Helen 35
Lovers Walk 110, 150
Lowden 9, 25, 39, 69, 100, 102, 112, 120, 161, 176, 177, 200, 206
Lowden Avenue 7, 192, 199
Lowden Hill 49, 67, 96, 101
Lowden Lodge 49
Lowden, Mayor of 9
Lowder, Alicia Eirene 106

Lowder, Amy 105
Loyalty Street 112
Loyalty Ward 129
Lysley, Gwendoline Matilda 124
Lysley, William 113
Lysley, William Lowther 124

M4 Motorway 88, 179, 198, 215, 216
Mackness, Frederick 158
Malmesbury Road 4, 36, 44, 57, 62, 68, 78, 103, 112
Market Place 15, 27, 32, 41, 48, 50, 58, 66, 77, 84, 85, 91, 99, 100, 101, 114, 116, 118, 124, 132, 134, 139, 146, 151, 156, 162, 170, 185, 191, 193, 198, 203, 212, 218
Marlborough Court 90
Marshall, Alderman 107, 108
Marshall Street 112, 212
Marshfield Road 11, 49, 56, 63, 83, 149, 199, 213, 214
Martin, George 64
Martin, Police War Reserve 51
Martin, Sid 172
Masonic Hall 93
Matthews, John 150
Mattingly, George 193
Maud Heath's Causeway 17, 96
Maxwell-Gumbleton, Canon 129
May, Barbara 7, 62
May, Michael 7, 62
Mayhew, Leonard George 190
McCann, John 144
McClatchie, Robert 127
McGuire, Patrick 27
Merryweather, Albert Edwin 19
Merryweather, Sarah Annie 19
Middlefield Adult Training Centre
Milestones 57, 68
Millennium Mural 21
Millennium Wall 166, 167
Millett, Canon John Desmond 171
Milsom, Harry 156
Milsom, William 180
Miners, Ernie 29
Minns, Myra 115
Minter, Eric William 109
Mitchell, William 64

Money, George 205
Monkton Estate 169
Monkton Hill 54, 98
Monkton Hill Methodist Church 145
Monkton House 106
Monkton Park 47, 85, 112, 114, 123, 140, 181, 210
Monkton Park Swimming Pool 76, 87, 133
Monkton Spring 39
Moore, Admiral Sir Graham 19, 36
Moore, Joseph 150
Moore, Mary Carrick 19, 20
Moore, Sir John 19
Moore, Superintendent 205
Morse, Mr & Mrs 140
Mortimer, Mr 126
Mortimore & Son, Messrs 29, 30
Mortimore, Peter 2
Moss, Gertrude Emmeline 179
Mountjoy, James 150
Mulocher, Maxence 37
Myall, Police Constable 55

National Union of Women's Suffrage Societies 116
Naylor, Marie 204, 205
Neeld Hall 13, 56, 74, 86, 96, 97, 118, 129, 170, 188, 203, 214
Neeld, Joseph 33, 146, 153
Neeld, Sir Audley Dallas 50, 74, 98, 182
Neeld, Sir John 100, 105, 113, 146
Nelson, Thomas 130
Nestlé's Condensed Milk Factory 2, 10, 36, 72
Nethermore 25
Newman, James 89
New Road 18, 52, 54, 78, 149, 152, 153, 213, 214, 221
Nicholls, William 159, 161
Norman, Mr 5

Pardoe, Emma Naomi 44
Pardoe, Jane 44
Park, Norman Edward 15
Parker, Miss 219
Pegler, Benjamin 4
Pew Hill 174
Pew Hill House 148, 149

Phipps, Captain 19
Powell, Albert 181
Powell, Charles 11
Powell, David 210
Powell, Enoch 77
Powell, Herbert 181
Pratt, David 218
Public houses;
   Angel Hotel 9, 15, 46, 113, 198, 210, 211, 218
   Bear Hotel 82, 116, 133, 149, 159
   Black Horse 52, 53, 145
   Five Alls 139, 140
   George Inn 2,
   Great Western Hotel 55, 56, 69, 125
   King's Head 113, 114
   Little George Inn 34, 79
   New Inn 97, 197
   Pheasant 97, 197
   Railway Inn 53, 93
   Rose & Crown 139, 140
   Rowden Arms 197
   Sun Inn 18
   Three Cups 196
   White Hart Inn 94, 192, 198, 209, 211
Pullen, Gertrude 7
Pullen, Victor 7

Queen Adelaide 151
Queen Alexandra 118
Queen Elizabeth II 91, 208, 209
Queen Elizabeth the Queen Mother 139
Queen Mary 72
Queen Mary (of Teck) 56, 137
Queen Victoria 9, 15, 19, 50, 100, 104, 184, 189

Radcliffe, Joan 93
RAF Colerne 43
Read, Alfred 130
Red Cross 129, 170, 176, 188
Reid Crow, Dr David 166
Revelation Christian Resource Centre 20, 21
Reynolds, James 150
Ricardo, David 65
Ricardo Road 141

Richmond, Mr 190
Rich, Rev. Canon John 9, 49, 169, 177
Ritchens, Albert 151
River Avon 53, 102, 133, 140, 147, 153, 157, 167, 221
River Lane (Common Slip) 221
River Street 20, 21, 27, 85, 137, 181
Roberts, Hilda 97
Robertson, Leigh 76
Robeson, Archdeacon 91
Robinson, Cubmaster 182
Rock Hole, The 148
Rooke, Mr & Mrs 74
Rooke, Wallace Mortimer 170
Rose, Annie 211
Rose, Nelson 210
Roseby's 108
Ross, Nigel 45
Rossiter, Police Detective 36
Rotary Club 59, 143
Roundheads 109, 117
Roundway Down 117
Rowden (Manor of) 108, 177
Rowden Farm 97
Rowden Hill 8, 17, 64, 92, 96, 151, 184, 213
Rowden Hill Cottages 185
Rowden Place 67
Rowden Road 102
Royal Indian Air Force 42
Royal Wiltshire Yeomanry 79, 140, 170
Rudman, Henry John 207
Rudman, Walter 182
Runnymede Memorial 43
Russell, William 79

Sadler, Police Superintendent 50
Sadlers Mead Car Park 8
Safeway 151
Sainsbury's 47, 128, 129
Salisbury 23, 24, 164, 168, 217
Salisbury Plain 25
Salvation Army 77, 91, 92, 141, 142, 158, 191, 194, 206, 207
Sarakcic, Mr 210
Sassy Ltd 122
Saunders, Anthony 175
Saxby & Farmer 49

Schools;
    Abbeyfield 68, 208
    Charter 167
    Chippenham & District Technical 47, 98, 168
    Frogwell 18, 167
    Hardenhuish 14, 33, 159
    Ivy Lane 5, 30, 56, 66, 167, 187
    Kings Lodge 167
    Langley Fitzurse 21, 165
    Lowden 8, 90, 107
    Maud Heath 165
    Monkton Park 96, 167, 187
    Redlands 167
    Sheldon School 109, 167
    St Andrew's National 6, 192
    St Margaret's Convent 8, 92
    St Mary's Catholic 8, 18, 92, 167
    St Nicholas 167
    St Paul's 58, 123, 124, 167
    St Peter's 167
    Westmead 14, 61, 115
Scott, George Gilbert 33
Scouts 181, 209
Self, Edwin Albert 4, 190
Seymour House Care Home 123
Shambles 18, 32, 179, 186, 196
Sheeley, Sharon 64
Sheldon Farm 154
Shell, Annie 168
Shell, Henry 168
Shepherd, Alan 216
Sketchleys 228
Slade, Caleb 126
Slade, Harry 16
Slade, William Goold 23
Slaughterford Mills 117
Smallcombe's shop 156
Small, Mayor 74
Smith, Albert 158
Smith-Dorrien, Sir Horace Lockwood 131
Smith, Gordon 14, 157
Smith, John 90
Smith, Kenneth 102
Snow, Rev. Philip 109
South, David 81
Southall, Christopher 147
Spar 18

Spear, Steve 57
Spencer, Arthur 116
Spicer, Anthony Napier Fane 194
Spicer, John 35
Spicer, Lady Avice 139
Spicer, Lady Margaret 129, 172
Sprules, Rose 97
Spurgeon, Charles 48
Spye Park 29, 35, 139, 172, 194
Stallard, William 129
St Andrew's Hospital 44, 91
Stanley Abbey 29
Stanley Lane 28, 29, 68
Stanley, Florence Mary 120
Stanton St Quinton 215
Starkey family 29
Station Hill 11, 38, 48, 100, 144, 152, 172
Sterling, Frances 116
Stevens, Arthur Moyle 13
Stevens, Charles Robert 178
Stevens, John 179
Stevens, William Ewart 7, 109
Stiles, Mr 55
St Mary Street 5, 112, 114, 117, 132, 158, 162, 170, 192, 221
Strong, Rev Thomas Augustus 34
Stroud, George 197
Suffrage Pilgrims 116
Suffragettes 204, 205
Suffragette's Retreat 205
Suffragists 116, 117
Summers, Charles 59
Summers, John 59
Summers, Mildred 59
Superdrug 108
Sutton, William 141, 142, 206
Sweeney, John 11
Swindon 10, 17, 58, 75, 79, 86, 88, 173, 195, 204, 205, 215
Swindon Cheese Supplies 122

Tadpoles 81
Tail-waggers Club 5
Talbot, Matilda Theresa 164
Tamlyn, Chief Inspector 171
Tavinor, Walter 134
Teagle, Gwendoline 202
Telephone Exchange 16, 138

Temperance Hall 15, 18, 19, 65, 144, 158, 204, 221
Terry, Ken 103
Tetbury Mail Cart 140
Thatcher, Cilla 103
Thatcher, Paul 103
The Range 154, 155
Thingley 197
Thingley Junction 10, 11, 25, 175
Thomas, George 150
Thomas, John 150
Thorpe, John 125
Thornton, Philomena 98
Thurston, Edward 123, 124
Timber Street 28, 45, 121, 148, 192, 198
Timbrell, Brian 102
Tinson, Frank 206
Tinson, George 206
Titanic, RMS 63
Todd, Jean 39
Toll houses and Turnpikes 64, 67, 68, 192
Tomes, Charles William 173
Tompkins, George 110
Tompkins, Patrick 64
Toogood, Police Constable 27
Town Bridge 2, 13, 18, 39, 51, 67, 72, 91, 119, 132, 134, 139, 140, 152, 158, 180, 181, 203, 210
Town Charter 72, 92
Town Clerk 169
Town Council 7, 36, 39, 40, 47, 50, 56, 73, 107, 111, 112, 121, 221
Town Hall 1, 2, 15, 43, 68, 74, 92, 129, 130, 133, 171, 172, 183, 188, 189, 202, 208
Town Pump 40
Townsend, Albert John 74
Townsend, Cora 93
Townsend, Julie 69
Townsend, Vera 97
Treleaven, Rev William Woodman 16
Trotman, Thomas Augustus 192
Trumpington, Baroness 62
TS Tiger 53
Tuck, Edward Newall 39, 107, 108, 133, 169, 179
Tuck, Sarah 212
Tucker, Rev Percy 21

Tugela Road 51
Turner, Arthur 219
Turner, Mary 219
Twelfth Night 5
Twinning 37
Two-Way Day 152
Tytherton Churchyard 50

Unidentified Flying Object 85
Union Road 190, 221
Unity Street 30, 112
Unity Ward 129, 130
Upton, Mr 78
Usher, Thomas Charles 105
Ushers Brewery 7
Utterson's Almshouses 176, 177

Van Diemen's Land 198

Walker, William 7
Wallace, Cecily May Poulett 1939
Waller 114, 117
Walpole, Robert, 22
Walrond, Eric 196
Warcup, Rev Alfred 178
War Memorial 66, 99, 124
Warrilow, Ernest Stratford 11
Warrilow, James Bakewell 11, 44, 78
Warwick, Robert 84
Waterford Mills 36, 82, 149, 165
Waters, Sergeant 211
Watson, Dr George 137
Watson, William 98
Watts, William 134
Waverley Hotel & Restaurant 116
Wavin Plastics 164
Way, Samuel 84
Webb, Doug 173
Webb, Israel 207
Webb, Lot 134
Webb, Police Constable 205
Webb, Sandie 167
Webb, Sylvia 176
Wells, Superintendent 194
West End Club 190
Western Arches 91, 141, 149, 150, 171, 213
Westinghouse 56, 70, 74, 77, 102, 120,

148, 149, 157, 208, 209
Westmead Lane 8, 44, 147, 165
West of England Cloth Company 80, 82
Weston, WH 176
West Tytherton 184
Whale, William 59
Wharf, The 68
Wheeler, Audrey 97
Wheeler, William 51
White, Ellen 126
White, George Alfred Huelin 126
Whitehead, George 216
Whiting, George 151
Whitmarsh, Harold 190
Wick Hill 17, 96
Wigmore, Harriet 98, 99
Wild, Reginald 29
Wildman, Aircraftman 1st Class 137
Williams, Mr 16
Williams, Mrs 57
Wilmot, Fred 129
Wilson, Margaret 39
Wilts & Berks Canal 26, 205
Wilts & Dorset Bank 67
Wiltshire Air Ambulance 33
Wiltshire Archaeological & Natural History Society 1, 42
Wiltshire Council 7, 143, 154, 177
Wiltshire Education Committee 7, 109
Wiltshire Police 7, 171
Wiltshire Regiment 66, 147, 170, 179
Wiltshire & Swindon History Centre 185
Winchester Three 144
Wood & Awdry, Messrs 78
Wood, Dr 117
Wood Lane 7, 14, 18, 32, 42, 51, 54, 79, 97, 108, 211
Wood, John (The Younger) 32, 187
Wood, June 57
Wood, Mr 24
Wood, William 27, 199
Woodlands Road 63, 90, 112
Woodman, John 150
Woods, Bernard 210
Woolley, Harold 75
Woolworths 3
Workhouse 73, 117, 120, 151
Wyndham Close 63

Yatton Keynell 131, 212
Yelde Hall 39, 40, 50, 72, 179, 180
Yeomans, Lila 115
Yewstock 4
Yewstock Crescent 4, 5, 187
Yoe-Stocks 4
Yorke, Colonel 11

www.ingramcontent.com/pod-product-compliance
Lightning Source LLC
Chambersburg PA
CBHW040319170426
43197CB00022B/2965